# HOIL

**By Iván Argüelles**

**Introduction by Jack Foley**

These poems are dedicated to the countless attendants, nurses and therapists who loved and cared for Max for so many years, and especially Vin Nguyen.

# HOIL

## An Unfinished Elegy
## By Iván Argüelles

### Introduction by Jack Foley

**Goldfish Press**
**Seattle**

Goldfish Press
4545 42nd Avenue Southwest
Suite 211
Seattle, WA 98116-4243

Manufactured in the United States of America

ISBN-13: 978-1950276028
ISBN-10: 1950276023

Library of Congress Catalog Card Number  2019943855

Book and Cover Design by Koon Woon

# Introduction

Iván Argüelles was born January 24, 1939. The brilliance of his verse has been demonstrated in a plethora of books pouring forth from him since 1978. There were influences—James Joyce, Ezra Pound, Jack Kerouac, Philip Lamantia and William Burroughs among them—but no one would mistake a poem by Argüelles for a poem by anyone else. The richness of the references sends us to the Internet, to encyclopediae, to old books, to foreign languages—above all to the Greek and Latin Classics, read by the author in the original tongues. "My mind was in flames," he remarked once, "multiplying in all directions." Argüelles' work is decidedly and deliberately *not prose* and offers the rare experience of a mapping of consciousness functioning at a peak of multiple associations. If at times it seems confused, confusing, it remains—even at its most opaque—elegant, eloquent. One might see it as a kind of 18th century "Neo-Classical" sensibility that has been subjected to all the horrors and ecstasies of the modern world—to that world's radical dissociations, ambiguities, and murderous intents. It is a huge lament for "Mind" as it once functioned but which the centuries have forced into an inferno of conflicts. "See what happens," Argüelles remarked once, "when they teach me to read!" Behind this outpouring—simultaneously chaotic and elegantly structured—lie Virgil and Dante with all the clarity their texts embody:

*Eurydicen vox ipsa et frigida lingua*
*a! miseram Eurydicen! anima fugiente vocabat:*
*Eurydicen toto referebant flumine ripae.*

*E'n la sua voluntade è nostra pace*    *

What happens when such a sensibility—a lamentation for the world of thought—encounters the anguished, immensely personal experience of grief? In the past few years Argüelles has suffered the loss of both his identical twin brother, the distinguished New Age figure, José Argüelles (1939-2011), and, more recently, his son, Max (1968-2018), afflicted since the age of ten with encephalitis and cared for in every sense by his parents. A lamentation that has incorporated the entire universe of language becomes, in addition, suddenly deeply personal and specific. The lamentation for thought is still there, but if these poems don't break your heart you have no heart to be broken. "Max's life," writes Argüelles, "was a mystery, a tragedy and a joy":

taken from the womb what was the gift?
I saw light and sparklers and heard
the boom of motor traffic out the window
cities came and cities went the biggest
where I lived knowing chalk and cement

bridges that seemed to fly and stores
filled with all the christmases in the world
glitter this and twinkle that basements
escalators subway trains and libraries
once I even went to see the Taj Mahal
and rode an elephant and slept in a bus
that zigzagged through the Himalayas
later on something happened a sore
in my mouth and fever and convulsions
what they call a coma a big red hiatus
between consciousness and chaos
as if an airplane had taken me and
swirling in a planet of clouds dropped
me down on a slope by a large water
where I lay for a long time suffering

Death speaks to poets, giving them words. None
finer than what we find in the lines of this
extraordinary American writer. Death and its
"outlet song of life" have been our theme since
Whitman. Here, song weaves grief into a stunning
music:

when does one start to die ?
imperceptible moments when the spirit
is totally absent and the world collides
with its own distance silent crashing
echoes redundant with whispers
from the beyond of light
edges disappear into boundless water

\* The voice itself and the cold tongue cried,
"Eurydice, ah, miserable Eurydice!" as life fled:
the banks of the entire river echoed, "Eurydice." (Virgil, *Georgics* IV)

In His will is our peace. (Dante, *La Divina Commedia*)


Jack Foley, 2019

# HOIL

*A PREFACE*

OUR SON Max died around 11 PM Feb. 28, 2018, abruptly it seemed, but not unexpectedly, in Kindred Hospital, San Leandro CA. After all, his had been an unusual and prolonged life, an existence that carried him to the reefs of consciousness back and forth many times. Born on Mar 9, 1968 in Nashville TN, he soon moved to Brooklyn NY where he spent the first ten years of his life with all the normal experiences and adventures of any boy of his era. He was basically happy and good natured. A few months after his 10th birthday Max became mysteriously and seriously ill, with symptoms that culminated in his being hospitalized and within a week he was in a coma and underwent several craneotomies. It turned out he had contracted a herpes encephalitis. For the next 40 years his was an epic of numerous ups and down, episodes of severe setbacks, but adventures of limited recovery as well, on horseback, in swimming pools, on a three wheeled bike, and with his electric synthesizer/piano which he loved playing above all. He remained at home, with the exception of numerous hospitalizations some quite lengthy, with us, his parents all this time. Until the end. Max's life was a mystery, a tragedy and a joy. Among the enigmas Max left behind was the word HOIL, a syllable he used to write on crayon drawings he made when he was a child around 5 or 6 years old. While we may never know what he meant by HOIL, these poems are an attempt to elucidate Max's death, as well as his life, giving some meaning it is hoped to the cosmic randomness that seemed to characterize his existence, HOIL!

It must be noted that while the poems here represent a concentration of *feeling* derived from a certain cosmic event, this is not a complete collection, as I continue and will keep on writing poems about Max, in life and death. For as long as I live the Universe will seem inconceivable without Max. HOIL!

*Candidus insuetum miratur limen Olympi*
*sub pedibusque videt nubes et sidera Daphnis*
                    *Virgil, Ecloga V, 56-57*

# *HOIL*

## *UNFINISHED ELEGY*

plum branch and yellowing grass
recall weaving in southern breeze
voices indistinct of summers passed
a toss of the dice a quarrel darkness
in the house on the hill a mystery
unresolved and faint the sounds
rising unexpectedly moon aspirin
transparent and large as heaven
crazy cloud mind weaving thought
earth tilts darkly far away leaving
this vast apparition lunar longing
casting a spell dissolving seasons
lifting tides of mind into labyrinth
gossamer white intricately blind
echoes of the very first echo dim
as water in its Minoan infancy
    *Max r.i.p.*

03-01-18


## *IN THE END WHAT LOSES MEANING*
## *ONLY TAKES ON GREATER SHAPE*

when does one start to die ?
imperceptible moments when the spirit
is totally absent and the world collides
with its own distance silent crashing
echoes redundant with whispers

**11**

from the beyond of light
edges disappear into boundless water
hand can hold nothing more
than the breath of air it takes
to release the body finally
from its desperate and inky contours
begins to die when the machine takes over
immaculate god of perfunctory routine
inevitable and inescapable logic
that defines without clarifying
what the mystery really is
the depths of soul trapped in growths
that no anti-biotic can cure
legend is a miasma of diagnoses
perceived through the contorted lens
of reason and *science*
angels appear at the windows
whirring wings of unbearable flame
come to take away what has been dying
all this time in its small shadow
in its brief memory of horse-back riding
of swimming of walking unaided !
what is all of history but a page
of smudged and erroneous ink
a fabrication of schools and flags
of aggravated nation states on the edge
when what has been dying all the while
is here and here as well in its puny
but beautiful attempt to focus
one last time on the shapes
of love hovering waiting
in anticipation

03-02-18

## MAX : A SHORT AUTOBIOGRAPHY

taken from the womb what was the gift ?
I saw light and sparklers and heard
the boom of motor traffic out the window
cities came and cities went the biggest
where I lived knowing chalk and cement
bridges that seemed to fly and stores
filled with all the christmases in the world
glitter this and twinkle that basements
escalators subway trains and libraries
once I even went to see the Taj Mahal
and rode an elephant and slept in a bus
that zigzagged through the Himalayas
later on something happened a sore
in my mouth and fever and convulsions
what they call a coma a big red hiatus
between consciousness and chaos
as if an airplane had taken me and
swirling in a planet of clouds dropped
me down on a slope by a large water
where I lay for a long time suffering
little but a headache the size of ink
to walk again I learned a bit and
to ride a horse listening to the wind
people immersed me in warm pools
and set me on a blue three wheeled bike
what a wonder the world was streaming
frontwards and back at the same time
half of what I understood was a language
missing most of its meaning or echoes
frequent and distant in the kaleidoscope
of my hearing until the convulsions returned
reversing my ability to conjecture light
for years that were a matter of days

**13**

or maybe weeks I kept on shifting slow
and at times falling too into strange holes
dark and impressions of endless nights
often winding up in hospital beds and
the machines blinking or bonking bright
like sirens moaning and crying to sleep
why I couldn't manage to get out of bed
without help to dress and wash and use
my left hand and so much else lopsided
to maintain my balance was good and to
actually stand and greet the new machine
music was wonderful to touch and sound
ringing like bells and to sing voicelessly
was my talent and I offered everyone
a handshake and joy even when I was
sliding off the cliff into a numerable abyss
into ways of consciousness that stuttered
OK it wasn't easy coming into the new
century with tubes and things that fastened
my shadow to electrodes pegged in the wall
I forgot how food tasted and my breath
became relentlessly out of rhythm
the ones I loved remained steadfast
and put me to bed and woke me up
tirelessly whether light or dark whenever
sometimes and suddenly the ambulances
came and took me back to crowded rooms
blinking and bonking and unconscious
for long periods dreaming I was a micronaut
in my plastic toy sailing the galaxies
trying with less success to stay awake
to breathe to keep up the heart's pace
until one day *this* day I ran into a wall
and all the noise and sparkling shimmer
stopped

*AVERNUS*

where does one go when the door shuts
are there windows inside or a trap-hole
hidden in the ceiling or secret words
to transport the soul to its next destiny
who fixes the length of the journey
or the route is it circuitous or direct
are there echoes from the former world
is there any familiarity in the furniture
or is there simply a darkened passage
and voices speaking unknown tongues
and lamps with flickering wicks and wax
running down into small brass dishes
does it feel like an ancient ruined temple
the feel of moss the scent of damp grass
blind statues representing the gods
of futility and longing and rusted arms
hanging on the walls and scraps of poems
in illegible scripts pasted to columns
fluttering in a rush of cold boreal air
does one know exactly where the exit is
or if there ever really was an entrance
it is easier to sleep again to forget what
it was that was being sought – a hand ?
in fact the body is now weightless more
like an unformed ink puzzled at motion
and gravity and the smell of dead flowers
does it levitate in a punctuation of hiatuses
are there question marks in its meridian
does a center exist floating between other
middle points in a jargon of stardust and
asterisks and when does it appear natural

to cease moving to rely on darkness for
memory of light thought and *others*
the mystery is inside the mystery enigmatic
oracular senseless to make meaning
everything is unfamiliar never felt before
treachery with endings and pitfalls
origins of the universe the many dotted
red and miniscule seem to flare up
and booming and iridescence of drums
always distant evoking seas of sand
islands where horses pasture on sunlight
wherever that may be and finally
the sound of smoke the silence of time
overtures of music that never begin
the soul at last taking its first steps
wingless birds in flight in the labyrinthine
nothingness of the unending voyage
above the fathomless lake of the afterlife !


03-03-18



## *ÜBER DEN TOD*

gone ! gone forever ! can one say
this is real just because another
step was not taken and yet joy
wrapped this face with incandescence
a pallor of light beyond light
to touch and not feel what is after
released from the bonds of memory
invisible Reality metaphysical What ?
we are and we definitely are Not

all at once surrounded by blossoms
bird song sunrise and sunset air
billowing all around and leaves
talking or silent at the windows
come out ! circle the garden !
just once more before sky takes
all its photographs away
silence is the greater part of time
so why make noise ? echoes
suffice in the now redundant ear
and the many prescriptions and
rules and provisos and caveats
don't do this ever again ! help
call 911 where's world-wide oxygen ?
sit down take it easy the keyboard
is at hand with its secret alphabets
music magical contact with elsewhere
or did all that happen yesterday ?
today is already three days disappeared
emptied of context wind ceases blowing
footsteps of the inaudible spirit
death invigorating and bountiful
opening its multiple door
swinging wide its floral portal
how great the Now-Beyond !
little voices smaller yet the hands
twice it asked and never heard
thrice and the hour struck its Bell
why do telephones exist if not
to convey the final message
you know how it goes
midnight and rain

03-04-18

**17**

*ARBOLITO !*

*arbolito !* this is not Ramayana
when a father can go no longer
into the light unbearable
when all about night beckons
and not come back to the house
to the bed the lamp and chair
to the small table in the dark
*arbolito !* the epic has not been
written of places long since gone
where a father must wake elsewhere
in a wood dense and labyrinthine
hearing an unrecorded music
of fixtures in time and space
vast and motionless galaxies
once the property of small hands
of eyes that scoured the Beyond
*arbolito !* my little tree of life !
punctuation ceases to mean
anything in the ineffable phrase
that follows complete silence
if a father can no more speak
but echo again and again
what never should have been
the sea outside the window
raising its arms to the moon
senseless as a cadaver of flame
that shifts its senseless red
into a world of frozen porphyry
*arbolito !* twice and thrice
the winds bore your shape
into the memory of grasses
mown on hillsides of the sun

**18**

which a father could not touch
but in sleep the deep unknown
what is today but the cancelled
autumn you never reached ?
what is tomorrow but wan
the pale effigy of your brow ?
*arbolito !* I planted you
yesterday in the furrow of
bright earth seed of myth
undefined eternal flowering

03-05-18


## AVE ATQUE VALE

of the ways the world has of being
none is more Mysterious than
its disappearance
what do Heraclitus and
Lucretius have to say ?
what can the Fathers of the Church
in their apologetics declaim ?
does sun flower best in China
and in Etruria lay its bed ?
of the all the worlds that can be
none is more enigmatic
than the disappeared
the one just inches from the light
the one removed from its axis
and laid to rest in Sicily
where Persephone was last seen
how does great Sun this day weep ?
and Moon pale sister decline her lamp ?

**19**

clouds bound all by a single thread
move their shapeless beauties
into the lesser field of gravity
space itself caught in Galileo's eye
becomes unadorned and small
as the single sand in Neptune's beard
smaller still than the moaning
unseen shadow of Zephyrus
why write poems of grief ?
whither are gone the Naiads
in their mourning damp of time ?
worlds no longer come and go
unless by invisible horses
pulled on fortune's dumb Wheel
into the dry well of emptiness
why indeed write poems of grief ?
words sounds noise echoes
all the decibels of silence
combined cannot make so much
sense as the absent vowels
and crushed consonants
that accent the hidden Voice
the one that forevermore
decries its missing World
and from balconies high above
the Piazza in ancient Rome
mothers ! mothers wail !

03-06-18

## THE FINAL PUNCTUATION

the next time the poem and all it implies
the sun and who governs the sun and its
heat circling in ever wider diagrams
around the illusory the flowering
the impending last day issuing forth
horses of black steel glistening which
are the breath and the engines of the
lungs and the thoracic cavity of Achilles
heroic vain and ultimately vulnerable
as all days are as all light is as all
everything including the poem its words
its silences the hyphen and the hiatus
the actual resonance like a vedic thought
crossing the Deccan and becoming fluid
or turning to steam and the enormous
above the poem lunar and corporeal both
heavens inch by inch annihilated by
Shiva or his look-alike and the universes
tumbling as in a washing machine poem
unintelligible as all human activity must
be ! poetry of the sliding scale of sands
and attributes of air bluish vanishing
higher than the last time and watching
carefully the needle on the screen shift
from red to ultra violet until the pulse
ceases radiating its imagination over
the map of Sri Lanka or Mozambique
wherever the human soul may digress
in its poetry of overcoming odds but
losing the battle the concord and sublime
to describe the poem as a belittled as a
small print at the bottom of the tractate

footnote or marginal vowels no voice can
utter without weeping and the shoulders
too and the swelling feet and the lymph
and the hemoglobin count what great sizes
one by one running ink into the foul play
if there were a Minerva or a Lucina
to guard the fluttering absences as they
pursue alternate routes over day's end
and the poem inside the telephone ringing
not answered not picked up and the lobby
with its antiseptic odor and paper plants
clambering up the edgeless and cosmic
yes , it is the final punctuation , the

03-06-18

## MAGNUM MYSTERIUM

is it in a blade of grass or in the pulse
missing from the wrist or merely
all the absences of sky in the shut eye
never mind the guttering taper
or the wafting temple perfumes
the murmur of voices gathered
in a small room to simply reminisce
what was once the shape of light
a human body the simulacrum of
music and speech gifts of Apollo
there is no greater mystery *they say*
than the peace that passes understanding
not in the leaf whose design imitates
a paradise of fifty summers nor
in the echo of a water running deep
beneath the immobility of time
remember ? tiny increments of red
horses tamed inside the Hour
regions of the sun where ink blossoms
words that have never been spoken
illusion that on the other side
of the window a new city grows
futile as is the longing to retrace steps
to return to the once and never been
to embrace without comprehending
why the shadow without form
here ! is this not the Hill ?
listen carefully for the unfolding
hold still until the crease doubles
don't touch just yet the lost breath
air is the supreme entity
air is the all encompassing

yet there is never enough of it
who can see where it goes at night ?
is it sleeping in the undelivered hand ?
forget what they told you about Sunday
there are other days of greater flame
pause before taking another step
the room with five walls is Now
the floor and the ceiling are One
you always knew that but were afraid
to tell anyone afraid to admit
that there is nothing left to know
whence the abyss of number ?
*magnum mysterium* life is the same
as death is the same as life
sitting there in the perplex of space
everything comes around in a rush
today was yesterday is tomorrow
rings of flowers edges of incense
smoke the invisible *corpus*
thou art that !

03-07-18


## THE MOURNING DOVE

who instructed the mourning dove ?
was it the muezzin of the clouds
whose early call doth fill the ear with sorrow ?
look far below the small pond
a paper boat sets sail to the other shore
I invite one and all to join the chorus
the farther bank turns red with light
and everything has its moment
and every moment has its soul
and every soul has its breaking point

who is not without a drop of sadness
who has not once heard the cry
the mourning dove in its intellect of feathers
the mourning dove in its farseeing death
who has not set his own paper boat
afloat across the sea of Being ?
dawn once more brings its tide of skies
its waves of fluctuating lamps
do we sleep in the arm of Grace ?
whose voice is so lost that to hear it
brings to a close the dream of life ?
look below once again the brief ditch
the inscribed bone within it
the hills that gather looking
for the seam that divides time from space
hearken ! the lone mourning dove
the iridescent rings about its throat
who taught it to coo so sublimely
who caressed it once so long ago
do you hear the whirring wings ?
not wings but the soul itself
one two and three times in its
circling Hour of eternity
come to rest at last

03-07-18

## LA VITA NUOVA

begins with the dying sun
the long lost western hills
beyond the reach of light
begins with giving up
the old book and poem
the ancient wild verdure
that dressed the questing mind
the envelopes of illusion
that brought every day its woe
begins with not speaking
to the loved ones gone
but illustrating their memory
with the fiction of a new life
the absent corridors
the lamps extinguished
by time's cold wind
begins with denying grief
holding back surreal tears
reaching out to invisible hands
and gripping the ineffable
begins with writing odes
to joy and effervescence
understanding the emptiness
at the root of all desire
realizing there are spaces
where no thought
can ever enter
begins with yes you know
just being around the corner
just walking loose down

the unpaved street
looking nowhere for the traffic
of a thousand dead cars
driven by blind angels
begins with of course
I'm OK just a bit you know
on this side of that
but otherwise what's the
difference between now
and the impossible then ?
begins with death
begins with death
afterwards only death
with its bright promise
of still another day

03-08-18

## COFFIN TEXT

the license plate was from another state
yet the passage was the same and minimal
from the distraught plain before the wall
to the unruly shore where boats rocked
back and forth in the nocturnal surge
too late for the embroidery already burned
the masses of bouquets turned to smoke
the body sent on its one-way mission
to some exquisite destination beyond flame
bewildered citizen and soldier alike stood
unsure of which direction to watch sky
as it turned slowly off its mercurial axis
oracular voices intoned puzzling sounds
language intended to be misunderstood
garbled phonetics of the gods a miasma
of uncoordinated syllables the Poem
passed from ear to ear in phantom sleep
how was one to know ? depths of red
sequences of echo diapason and meter
linked to something fainter yet from
outer space and the text too fragmented
letters squiggles dots commas asterisks
finger pointing to opposite sides of the
whatever could not be read illegible
seas of ink assuming human form or
simply existing in an imperfection as
sublime as it was uncoordinated loose
things failing their sense and abysses
opening to other abysses below the mind
that purports to comprehend the Whole

**28**

underneath everything the string of words
the abstract assortment of dream vowels
pillow muffled sections of cloud fogs mists
and the rain the constant and unending
where cliffs abruptly conclude prayers
ineffable portions chapters about what
can never be deciphered and on either
side of the lid appeals entreaties weeping
what deity could listen without kneeling
helplessly in his Olympus of utter ruin
what is that mortal sound ? whose small
fiction is meant to matter in the blaze ?
bird cat dragon wolf demon basilisk
each with their symbol and three-headed
dog and swarming ants dizzying bees
the other universe ! painted for a moment
only then lured by fate into destruction
all memory of tongues and thought
gone ! little by little the signs vanish
no more the designing hand nor the eye
all-encompassing in its futile heaven
nothing but an alphabet of ashes
SHANTI OM
*for Max on his 50$^{th}$ birthday*

03-09-18

## HOMO FUGIT VELUT UMBRA
### ... bisogna morire

do I read these letters aright ?
one two and three have been cancelled
the next flight leaves yesterday at thirteen
gods who otherwise have been forgotten
reappear at the top of the stairs
each with their own cigarette fingers
atremble hair scattered to the breeze
mountaintops quivering in early light
*Night !* sequence of punctuated
stars like powders shaking in the aftermath
of a spent life-force illusory math
of the cumulated days of an endless summer
see ! sparrow leaf and pebble painted
disorder and chaos of the unseeing eye
echoes and then abruptly the silence
of cliffs erected overnight by a hand
shaped like a sky of invisible inks
tell me it isn't so ! signs wavering
in directions that none can follow
wood and vale and chastened grass
haunted underbrush and shadows
whispering here was a man passing
a fellow traveler in the music of time
you know him ! a son a brother a phantom
a wraith of poetry waiting to be recited
tombstones instead like massive stone vowels
etched in the bluish air names missing
from the registry of archaic myth
a voice issues from a torn branch

**30**

a language an idiom a phraseology
of hieroglyph and shifting sand
red is triumphant ! missives spears
arrows volleys of gunshot the ear !
wherever a writing has occurred
whenever a script has ventured to say :
the universe is a conflagration !
mortals have no say in the outcome !
so be it yet random letters scattered
across the dream of being spell nothing
we are still here for a day it seems
we are watching and waiting
for the unfolding of primordial sounds
for syllables that cannot be heard
why do you weep ? this Hour too will end
*bisogna morire*

03-11-18


ORACLE BONES

mind flight nocturne invisibility zero
who will play and who will regret
finally a sky without seams a cloudless
eye fills with decisions lacking form
an instant in the yard yellow weeds
others looking on absent soulless
whose shadow is that climbing the wall
so much has passed beneath a leaf
alone the longing of a last breath
moving eternally from words unsaid
silence is the greater part of the ear
listening doesn't correct the inky hue

**31**

covering the rocky soil of memories
who hasn't recalled the moment
when possibility of return was denied
great houses emptied of their carrion
smaller units of thought become red
isolated in fragments of space shifting
always toward the left the inert head
was once the deposit of light , yes !
one by one the steps up the ramp
a hand wavering becomes immense
the shape of an undetected galaxy
how much in that small refrain above
singing a voice that has not learned
as statues to speak with any clarity
one day it will be understood aloud
though none on earth will hear it
you and I it always seems in dialogue
but what we say is broken by a noise
carrying with it unbearable nostalgia
unrecognized we scour the mirror
for the face we thought we knew
the departed the brief lamp of joy
how many years did it take to know
only to lose it irrevocably unheard
tomorrow is but an inch of time gone
that bears no resemblance to this Hour
talk ! from what profound depths
sleep ! forget what it was that hurt
flesh like marble lifted into infinity
the beauty of a moment in paradise
air billowing atmospheres vanishing
night again the ineffable Unknown

03-12-18

## CREMATION

neither good nor bad have you foreseen
immortals ! nor on earth nor in the skies
luminous or nocturnal does justice rule
all is a random pivot off the axis eternal
things of beauty of delicate proportion
of skin merging with song of shadow
tracing echo in longing and disappearance
what was the gift ? what was the summer
of leaf and grass if not the burden to
endure the unexpected fever the downpour
the figure isolated in glass the torment
no love could bear what was that immortals ?
a sargasso of tenuous fragments littered
across the eye's night sky and sleeping
in the irregularity of an unpunctuated
paragraph the length of ink the duration
of sand the inexplicable and yet gorgeous
moment when things come together only
to turn chaotic in the following minute
let us count the seconds lets us enumerate
the years that lapsed between the one
and the other of the many and the none
alphabets of indecipherable texts of heat
of cycles of destruction of renewals without
hope of whatever else the human heart
tries to fathom but fails and the color
red instantaneous epic behind eyelids
shutting a last time on the unthinkable
come ! what are the forms on the wall
but lost identities nameless memories

escape routes to the chasm of the Unknown
when were we ever really Here becoming
and ceasing to exist revolving like suns
in the plenitude of an invisible cosmos
and in the afternoons in greek restaurants
they talk of deliverance and salvation
and the Logos and the incontinent Mind
and outside in the plaza automobiles shine
people traffic back and forth like museums
of recollection and destiny witless artifacts
talking statues animated stone to one another
unrecognizable and pass from this life to
the next blank philosophical conjectures
but you my Love ! the manifest and One
hold me and bury me in your rosy folds
oblivion of the immortals ! that we
have ever been in the here and now
that is the great illusion and to forget
simply to forget our burning desires
*as smoke we rise into the infinite*

03-13-18


*EPITAPH*


his boyhood face his light blue skin
can't bring him back he's gone for good
on his sled driving through distant snows
four years old or fifty what's the difference
the house is missing the smoke unwound
heavens in the air his small kite flew
hop skip and jump on sidewalks painted
for their brief antiquity he seemed to lift
no weight all tousled hair a breeze he was

**34**

unseen yet moving as if through grasses
a plaything all arms and legs bare to the sun
come back no more his winsome smile
burning lonely through so many clouds
a mountain climber into valleys he dove
gone forever so they say an infant
a boy a corpse bereaved in silks
his boyhood face his light blue skin
can't bring him back he's gone for good

06-11-18


## THE LAST GOODBYE

weary from often repeated going
back was it afternoon or morning and
forth circular heat visions of many lives
the one life that mattered evening's
turn to repeat hours on the uncounted
quicksilver rotating around the heart's
solar disk the greater wheel and the lesser
which is the one to cling to whirling out
of mind prose fabrications of circles
gyres and always the goal to find switches
on or off returning before the hour's
weekly visits to memory's gravesite
unable to identify the footsteps and
the ear and the device that puts into
motion fears and anxieties reverting
to some unidentifiable starting point
objects plummeting down from where
someone else is calling us back to go
not there take the next turn to the

right follow the thin strip of white
indistinct formations the alpha and
skip the betas a forewarning gamma
always iota and omega shifting into
enormous red galactic shapes of past
time days out of sorts like gravel pits
mysteries of glass and sunsets more
random than gold striating  windows
a beckoning finger to come back
to a corner of space limited access
mourning the accidental flash that came
and went wasn't that a mirage an echo
of light the evanescent punctuation
cannot grasp the meaning in the end
fossil shadow levitating from earth
its hand gone inert writing *goodbye*

06-14-18

*BUTTERFLY*
      *for Marilla*

was our butterfly he was and now flying
free of the mortal cocoon to think of him
wings dusted off all but transparent
in the light eternal living from flower
to flower in a world we couldn't give him
beyond the words for home and mother
soaring delicately in spheres of glass and time
try to imagine his flight pattern traced
in invisible inks his multi-faceted eyes
come back no more to this war-torn earth
other moons attend his new nights
other stars wake him in the midst of infinity
shapeless yet gorgeous patterns of breath
luminous deities his mind emits hovering

**36**

statues of galactic dust without memory
at his side reminding him nevertheless
that a body he once was a fugitive from birth
tormented for a few brief human years
by a life he never asked for a realm
he scarce could comprehend shifting across
calendars no more useful than desert sand
our butterfly he was and is flitting
in and out of the instant we call mortality
flying away from the labyrinth of thought
our tenuous fragile immortal butterfly

06-15-18


## CONJECTURE OF EXISTENCE

      in the decay of our years
the past gone forever out of hand
slipped like a shadow through water a
sleeping absence a phantom wavering
no poem can retrieve no lyric bring back
small white petals taken by the wind
asunder in the vanishing evening sky
lesser still and infinitely briefer stars
glittering in the brain's puny outback
this carefully constructed chaos like
a pinwheel out of control blazing
through all the hemispheres of space
this infinitesimal inch of breath
called mortality its failing decades
its lunations of parenthetical light
its histories curtailed by ampersands
and commas that delineate nothing
what words ! we succumb to lies
that a future awaits those who die

**37**

that a wilderness called paradise lies
far ahead with primrose dalliance and
whatever else the human mind conspires
to deceive itself with gardens and parks
sublime poetries angels living statues
that revive dreams talking out loud
in a language none can ever understand
what ear ! sands that fill the beyond
and pharaohs that walk on stilts of sound
through the enormously blank vocabulary
that feeds our vacant thoughts
what minds ! two plus two the end
of childhood three times three death !
to satisfy the dream of immortality
reckoning with this fading alphabet
lost syllables of unending silence

06-18-18

*CONDOLENCES*

still it says another day and a card comes
in the unsuspecting but as usual condolences
so much time can have elapsed though
it's no more than eight minutes since we
marked the end of childhood with sepia print
cutouts of memory on a fly-leaf overview
small red things floating in the mists of
exactly when and where we'll never come
to grips with the truth as grief is so polyvalent
and irrational as to leave no dots behind
only the occasional stains longing and hours
that turn into parking lots the vast empty
ones after twilight when the surrounding
hills gather to confirm a light has been
that will return no more and hush the grasses

slender the leaves beating their tiny hearts
against the cement folios of what is left
behind the others trailing their linens
what can be a sadder sight the folded cloth
with no references to its purpose smoke
vertiginous and wasted scrawling a signature
in the violet aphasia of evening before distance
itself takes the useless metal vehicles into
an even more remote rust can you hear
the voices echoing ?

06-25-18

## THE LORDS OF HELL

hidden in the grass waiting for the kids
to come home from school many an afternoon
only the shadows were missing and the trees
all around gathered like protective spirits
great the spreading lawns and the houses
behind the striped awnings and to the south
the generous hills capacious as smoke
and everywhere at times the vertiginous hush
eternity rippling in the burgeoning summer sky
a hint of death the terrific finger of fate
trembling like lightning in the clouds
unfelt as of yet and capricious innocence
spreading across the terraced field to the pool
sacred to nymphs long forgotten and to the sun
about to seize at a whim the bodies diving
in and out of the water's random arroyos
texts of echo and leaf and rock the hour
of time it takes to involve and dispose of a life
turn to look and *Behold !* the stranger
enticing as a god attending the refreshment
stand as if it were the temple of Diana herself

**39**

the huntress striding in her wanton gaze to kill
unawares the lithe and lissome spotted deer
in whose darting eyes the capsized world
seemed to smolder with a distant heat
how perfect the moment was a vacation of
hues and sounds revolving in the drowning ear
*come home no more !* in each twist of weed
or crunch of gravel implicit death guileless
as a schoolboy spending idle hours bereft
of thought a mind no larger than a pebble
white and lost in an avalanche of memories
that can never be reconstituted small sections
of distance fading in the puerperal fever
brought on by a momentary desire to *see*
what lies beyond the forbidden canopy of sky
waning light of outlined bodies humming bird
butterfly and angels no longer visible
followed by clouds of fireflies sparkling
a light a loss a leaf a blade a drop of water
weightless monuments of oblivion's fade

06-29-18

*MICRONAUT*

from depths that never quite see into the green
again nor the blue alternative to sky unconscious
as visible stars may be you lay there inert
receptacle of the most improbable dreams
teleportations to lunar crevices where deities
of everything white assumed shape and rains
phosphoric and intermittent from planet X
tattooed a poetry on your skin's underside
whatever you tried to convey to us whatever
language you were trying to use without
vowels or consonants in an epic struggle to widen

**40**

the scope of communication the most beautiful
forms of summer echoing in the thousand and
one leaves of the tree of life that grew in the vertigo
of your memory and how little we understood
of your protean maze zigzagging through space
the negative curvature to the other side of time
so many questions we had to ask but could not
does air have teeth ? can the jaguar in your eye
leap back into its shadow ? which is the direction
south ? are the dead so tiny and unimportant ?
what is the function of Y ? why does this week
have to last forever ? you fixed everything in
your redundant fists and answered nothing
without first checking the asterisk and the lung
and hand to throttle your little engine took off
for forty years we wondered if the shirts still fit
if the shoe on the left really belonged on the right
if the music we heard coming from behind
the empty mirror only happened at three AM
try as we might to locate the backside of sand
and to listen for the murmur of the river that
runs underneath the eyelids of your small library
polishing repeatedly the inverted glass with
its image of a kite flying endlessly above Prospect Park
and to put on that pair of pants over your legs
but they were running too fast moving like
dust over the mountain that defines the end of all
how could we believe anything the doctors said about
mercurochrome or the division of x-rays into wind
there was only a tumult of windows and names
too scientific and disproportionate for your age
you knew what we will never know about water
its various dimensions are like nameless months
running on over the insoluble mind of reason
you aloft for so long in your midget space craft
waving your invisible hands goodbye to cafeterias

waiting rooms curtains and gadgets that measure
heat and hair and weight and the imponderable
size of distance your shy elusive smile the key
to the great invertebrate thought of the Unknown

07-01-18


## THE FAR-SIDE OF THE UNIVERSE

the immense vast too empty to fathom
yet no greater than a leaf or a butterfly
the size of forty nine summers condensed
into a single blade of grass now withering
yellow enormity of chaos caught for the last
time in a glance of breathless panic
to live ! certainly for the few final hours
of light and running back and forth with
thermometers reading the charts the ding
dong ringing of alarms saying *this is it*
cosmos returned to its weightless cradle
a purge of countless Black Holes riddled
in quantum theory and the sheer inability
to count backwards once the switch is off
what was it all about the bicycle and kite
the torn pant-leg the shoe that won't fit
Saturday mornings idling in basement stores
in search of the perfect toy the plastic robot
able to fly off into outer space and be back
by noon just in time for the last ambulance
learning to die in a minute's time and return
revived by transfusions and new anti-seizure
medications and always and forever the pet
thought the isolated window the unturned corner
couldn't come back that way couldn't speak
anymore couldn't articulate the puzzlement

loss anomie grief aphasia dereliction confusion
how inflated the earth's atmosphere has become
aggravation of clouds and compromised sun
how many streets can be remembered trains
clarinet lessons trans-atlantic flights taxis
wild vivid rides distorted profusions of faces
voices coming out of crevices and cracks
balloons rising improbably out of hands
that no longer hold and mechanical sounds
inches of darkness taking over and silence
the far-side of the universe instantly red
brighter than anything for just a second
and immediately enormous vast and empty
the transfigured dot absorbing everything
to die ! *Max* come full circle now low tide
riding out to the depthless sea

07-06-18

*THE GREAT PHASE OF DEATH*

what is living but the exercise of dying
sunlight nothing but the darkness of the tomb
what is the short end of the day but night's
endless shift starless loss of moon and thought
what is it we are caught doing if not postponing
the moment we are all waiting for the luminous
ultimate abracadabra of the great secret
nothing can be transmitted back nothing
can be translated of that enormous enigmatic
script which we struggle at deciphering daily
let us celebrate the great phase of Death
does this mean we remain forever helpless
in the myths of our great poetries mere masks
acting out preordained roles suffering oblivion
will the body ever understand what the mind does ?

**43**

on either side of the camp pitched tents fires
ballista prepared to fling as far as lunacy permits
sword and rope and unpaired shoes and fear
the commas and juxtapositions of language
the blazing ampersand and bristling asterisk
the heavens unfurled with their burning silks
gods in sudden amaze at their own short lives
threads cut at the base and hairline denied
seas come running up to receding shores
sands beg for a repulse of the brevity of space
time stands on a single foot imbibing air
until there is no more to go around
oxygen in short supply lungs out of control
the soldiers who are the children of children
crawl into beds no larger than nails or tacks
fleas lice termites flies and worst of all bees
swarm the atmosphere to claim supreme domain
remember the time you were dreaming angel
and flight among the clouds and rainstorms
and furious summer abodes in tangled ivy
you were never going to wake from that dream
exchanging hands with willing strangers
taking steps on your own moving swiftly
through crowds of those dispossessed of breath
enormous the possibilities of a single night
dreaming you were still alive and shaping
worlds that lasted for a minute and a day
happiness and legends of golden infancy
alas the numb and moaning solitude in sheets
no greater than a thumb and the little lamp
and the shuttles that ceased working above
your head that immense labyrinth of thoughts
now forever stilled and the leaf outside the glass
the archaic wind that belongs only to the trees

07-08-18

## THE LOST HAPPINESS

in the mail it said you'd be a little late
the famous western skies of ochre and jasmine
beginning to set on their Umbrian mountain
small scudding clouds like briefly gloved hands
waving through the partial network of trees
holding their own arms high reaching for
the persistent vowel that shapes so much of sleep
the least shudder of a breeze welcomed
the rotating darkness left by the day's heat
everything was as they say picture perfect
could hear the on and off humming of motor traffic
through half-opened windows and the fragrance
of lilac and something else indefinable
made the head drowsy with longing waiting
by the empty table where only an hour ago
thunder and hail had played a last game
of checkers in a dream sequence of a lost summer
threadbare Nymphs came and went serving tea
a voice from upstairs boomed railing
against the current government and the rattle
of newsprint and garbled radio voices
what else to remind us of the world ?
we were no more of it than we were of sand
and its tumultuous and somnolent empire
waiting for the clock to strike watching
shadows make a universe of distance on the wall
listening for some footsteps or the creak
of a winch or a wheel or the snap of the sail
something of your return from that long voyage
you took four months ago but now only
the snapdragons drooping and an iteration
of crickets in their dusky china of spreading ink

what are one two and three what is the nail
maintaining the crack in the plaster
what has anything to do with anything
fireflies and silhouettes of forbidden planets
looming in the already past midnight of time
hearing a lost happiness echo off into waves
sad imitation of your voice in far off waters
like memory going to sleep in the lone ear
gone the leaf and its small rustling
color of silence pale a fade a

07-08-18

## THE TRANSCENDENT LIFE

tender is the leaf more tender still
the vanishing dew and the face it contains
paper transactions signatures and oaths
binding and unbinding treaties in the stars
signs and the distant roaring of the cosmos
born on earth and raised in the mirror of time
come and gone in the instant of recognition
the self at play in the meadows of oblivion
where great conjectures riddle the mind
about distance and direction and purpose
where is the child that can withstand
the indivisible scrutiny of the doctors ?
sweet is the light and sweeter still the air
all surrounding with its concourse of shapes
like planets rushing through the rapt eye
to be able to seize and hold just one of them !
the days pass and the nights that stubbornly
hold sway over the months of the year
until the moment arrives when the sheet
of abstract infinity is spread like ether
over the uncomprehending body

where is there to look so many windows
to see rushing the transcendent life
with its swiftly diminishing wings set flight
seeking other houses other lawns
woods and coves and grassy slopes beyond
the routines of memory and longing
what is to account for the sudden loss ?
echoes follow the calendar's blank pages
mornings dawn and the long siege of daylight
repeated as if a gift of the gods
prolonging a life without substance
immeasurable mourning in the clocks
that relentlessly count untimely absence
*fragile as it was the single blade of grass*
*was immense for the joy it gave*

10-11-18


## ELEGY FOR MY WIFE

no longer able or willing to count the earth
without fingers the gossamer piled on high
cloud loom distances of hazy dun hills worn
from viewing the eye caters to the soul and
the soul is gone from its solitary parapet
wont to weave its ink-tinged dreams a sadness
can these years amount to so little a bitter
accent on the elongated vowel and tinfoil
addressing the nation of sky within the eyelid
some voices stammer between the lashes
a sea with all its infinite roaring at the glass
a sliding note glissando on the taut wire that
extends from the origins to the still point
just above the edge of paper writing declares
to be void as are the enormous trajectories

**47**

of sleep from planet to planet I am spent
of living and the experiences of an afternoon
lodged between the ampersand and its discus
a blow to the weary of head and dizzying lapse
can almost hear the ambulance the tires wet
on the paving stones enumerated for saints
and the fierce decision to give it up the body
recounts in the small shell it travels in going
up the celestial flue among the wraiths who
distribute memory and the myths attendant
on the city here that's where we are right now
mowers and sirens and decrepit store-houses
of knowledge and tatters of consonants built
to keep out the storms entire lives in rhyme
and the echoing hollow sensation that ends
before it begins I know you from somewhere
I know those lips a carmine intensity the night
we are together for the last syllable a warning
in the lamp a seditious and tremulous hour
at hand the vacancies are posted and finally
the world such as we knew it the movie houses
the abandoned lots the elevated highway and
its river opaque greenish in the sullen fog
did we grow up there were the children sized
for language and cut their hair and clipped
et cetera the nails the shirts turned small frayed
as they were themselves off the margin a sound
can never forget that moment less than seraphic
gave up the toys and cutlery hidden sashes a
ribbon meant as a reward and the fluttering
agonizing really we rushed around in circles
earth had lost its historical basis and we wept

07-11-18

## BENEDICT DRIVE

the hand held last the rays of light gone
midnight and silence the news from planet X
just in with its tangle of ivy and distance
budding leaves and the fringe of air necessary
for the following day if only and the exits
marked in small Greek epistles who could
ever find the way back through all that
a rain and phalanxes of windy darkness
the gods kept their remove from the empty
whatever life had kept of its reservoirs
was gone like the other paraphernalia
of myth and journalism and the combs
and toothworks and delicate skin creams
do things turn dusk so swiftly like the hills
through which the mind must travel
looking for sleep for the antidote to sunlight
exhausted the limbs become clouds billowing
in the soft terrain of the imagined moon
lunacy of cadavers and rolling dust forms
poetry without words and levers and winches
elevating thought if possible to another floor
of the incomplete structure of the body
a longing to dissolve the present forever
if only to maintain of the past its rock
formations its sandy bulwarks its love
in the shape now of only a shadow missing
between the walls and the misinformation
of breath and allusions to cognition
lovely meadows where the sheep in the eyes
used to roam the lengthening twilight
which becomes ultimately a mountain
marble fractions of sky and a prescription

**49**

for an anti-biotic the last of its kind
flowering in the tissue of melancholy
how came we to this disorder ?
the steering wheel maintains its rights
driving through all the unanswered roads
that take us back to the small and unformed
house where it all began a dense
dreaming sequence of hives and avenues
the city that exists nowhere on the map
hands fingers anesthetic translations
of the irretrievable silence

07-13-18

*SAINT MAX*

great and splendid the mornings when
in your magic chair you greeted the first light
and the glorious Egyptian priests invisible
in their spotless white linen intoned
with hymn *"Ha Pepi Pu"* the rising orb
and with joy bush herb grass tree leaf
beloved of bug and bird alike you blessed
by your mere presence and even the concrete
resounded with secret thrill of companionship
all the elements in the cosmos air and azure
ether cloud and spark glistening as if
in tune with your secret emanations of life
the epic struggle to overcome obstacles
and when you reached your happy hand forth
to greet and bless the homeless and hungry
who in their morning passage came to you
a benediction in their grateful smiles
an entire orient of speechless admiration
in their eyes rejoiced by sight of you firm
in your intention to take the day's first steps

**50**

the street still damp from the celestial night
as if rising to watch your sweet presence lift
and move however shaky cane in hand
down the holy walkway to the goal
and back again determination and grit
fiercely imprinted on your innocent face
features the earth will not soon forget
now that we have separated your body
from the spirit inherent in your every gesture
and the most of you has flown seraphic
and weightless into the upper atmospheres
where those return who on earth have accomplished
more than was expected of them like you endowed
soul who at every turn of the screw persisted
giving in return to others felicitous surprise
joyous tribute of breath and the light
that only eyes that have *seen* can render
none whom your indomitable presence touched
can ignore memory of that contact itself
proof of a life few will ever fully understand
*Saint Max* who never did ill nor harmed
in the passing of so many tumultuous hours
any being but instead shed a brief lamp
on the world's darker mysteries
if only for the instant it takes to alter
night into everlasting day

07-14-18

*THE INDECIPHERABLE LIFE*

not the lifetime that was offered
but the one that was taken away
and to name mountains and force
illusions into their cloud-frame and
come together over the little memories

**51**

of sleep and the longing to endure
for just one more day the light
rendering the whole of a life
sample of water sand and filtered
oxygen and the talking going on
between phantom agents of twilight
and the hills it represents the dusk
can one ever get over the stubborn
horizon and the odor of burnt trees
and recollections of shores otherwise
disappeared from the map the mind
retains of a childhood in splendid parks
a music of lattice and trellis and heights
suddenly the fixity of a thought
discovered in a library down the road
smaller details of growing up and vague
the stores with their bright awnings
and the basements of rusted fobs
and plumbing parts and delusional
sections of time readjusted and simplified
so going to bed is less difficult and
trying to forget as always what went
before the light faded on the wall
a hand looking for its ink and fingers
tracing trajectories of distant cities
half recognized and the numinous
planets that bring on dreams
to think that history has come and gone !
myth of the earliest golden age
legendary creatures of rock and grotto
nymphs with glistening damp hair
combs and pellucid ornaments and
a single word that opens gates
paradise in the pocket of sky
to the far upper left called Olympus
and then the downpour of summer rains

the aggrieved lawns the muffled
echoes of things vanishing from scope
each of us behind a mirror
searching for the outline or shadow
of an identity we thought was our own
peculiarities of the mind drifting
as ever closer to the final moment
trousers and shirts and shoes
by which we identify who it was
that we were looking for but could
never find the *enigmatic soul*
was it in pursuit of this love
that we spent our days ?

07-17-18


## THE PASSING MYSTERY

come and gone between parentheses
breath and light now become memory
the pulse in the leaf the short breeze
winding itself around the sapling
tremulous blades of grass shooting up
near the rock and the well and the shade
a monument of invisibility and hours
spent listening for the sea to come up
as far as the unfinished brick wall a
silence between the references to myth
to the unfelt passage of things without
substance like thoughts of air or clouds
the entire cosmos gravitating in a dew-drop
toward the still point when night dissolves
and the future once so imminent is
nothing but the foregone past a whispering

**53**

somewhere in the gravel or the dolorous
sensation of a life an actual potentiality
in a summer that lasts a matter of minutes
heat and the vibrations of distance
in the far off hills of a legendary February
smoke and the resistance to matter
the sun itself shaking in the tumultuous
course of his horses racing beyond
the goal posts and the frequent mountain
like a world of feathers turning purple
in the declining lamplight of eternity
somewhere a writing persists in pale ink
a tale of hair and hands and feet
running in the dusty embolisms of mind
a creation of names and a purpose to overcome
obstacles of wave and sand and fever
endless circling in the solitary confines
of skin and words a lengthening twilight
of language and meaning a sign the size
of red in the hallucinatory galaxy that
dwindles no sooner does it reach a capacity
for space in the enormous reaches where
light still remains the only possibility
all else is an incomplete history of identity
the baffling enigma of birth and death

07-18-18


THE PURVEYOR OF SOUND

who governs the rock ? who dresses the vine ?
who colors the wind carving signs in the air ?
who names the child and grieves ? who aims
the dart pining for the pelt ? who sets the foot ?

**54**

who shifts the hand ? what is the world symbol ?
where does water get its shape ? who made heat ?
why does grass murmur in the night ? am I
the sole purveyor of sound ? where does time
go when the door shuts ? who are you then ?
who dyes the mind ? who traces dew ? who cuts
the finger from its joint ? who pierces the root ?
who clothes the child and weeps ? who says the hour ?
who fixes the day ? who calls the name ? who
knows the eye ? who drills the hair ? who pales
the ear ? why do leaves bleed ? who speaks
for the knee ? who weighs the shoulder ? who
kisses the lip ? who prays at midnight ? who bites
the tongue ? who peels the bark ? who loves
the worm ? who laces the shoe ? who paints the wall ?
who leads the child home sighing ? where is space ?
how many is number ? who talks to the comb ?
who are the zero ? what letter comes second ?
who counts the echoes ? who sets light in the glass ?
who emerges from the cloud ? who sleeps in the child ?
who wakes in the well ? who pronounces the moon ?
who puts ampersands in thunder ? who goes
when I cannot ? who determines the end ? who
writes the poem ? who understands nothing ? who
is the grammar of the afternoon ? who is the library ?
where is last month ? who says it is summer ?
who waits for the blackboard ? who dreams of chalk ?
who shakes out the dust ? who buttons the shirt ?
who rings the alarm ? who has lost the child ?
who can answer the window ? why is it ancient ?
who is the god at the top of the stairs ? where
is there to turn ? who scratches the cheek ?
what is in the basement ? who dares to move
among the syllables ? who owns the vowel ?
who measures the pulse ? who has the key to the sky ?
who can say why there is so much ? who remembers

so little ? who dives into the pool ? who does not
return ? who is the child missing in the alphabet ?
who takes off his socks ? who pays for the consonant ?
who keeps forgetting why ? who keeps forgetting why ?
why does smoke stand still ? who presses the button ?
who removes the thought ? who sits crying in the dark ?
who is in the painted box ? who suffers the inch ?
am I the sole purveyor of sound ?

07-20-18

*THE BROKEN SYLLABLE*

how could we know Wednesday would be the last
now all Wednesdays are conflated into one final
dissonant dislocated vowel a remoteness of gravel
flung into a wet breeze and all the archaic words
that accompany it wood brook glen mountain trees
grass rock slope sand and stone to name a few
sounding the wounded air with almost a sweetness
cannot bear to remember that tomorrow is Thursday
already and that the call will be out to those whose
concern is the dead and their clothing and fittings
that a new wind will usher in the now ancient sun
how much has happened in a matter of minutes
holding up to the lamp the skeleton of breath
while the fossils that bear night away into its cavity
one by one grow dim leaving only a difficult silence
in their wake a moistened but invisible finger tracing
a symbol in the fractured letter that lingers where
a whole word used to be just hanging in the air
of the now abandoned room what will we name it
a difference of time zones a relic of the orient
where we tarried once in a mausoleum of marbles
shattered for the fragility of their haunting beauty
moonlight between the commas and a perfumed

solace a bereavement in darkening consonants
a language that can no longer be spoken because
it is Wednesday all over again on the stopwatch

07-25-18


*EVENING THE FADE OF ALL*

the spine still hot from fever
yet already walking barefoot
in grasses wet with dew distilled
by the sun now an opaque orb
declining in the western hills
a myth of life and breath and
the great and fortuitous guesses
about light and the origins of time
and given the small space for the
soul to escape and the multiple
days of water left in the pool
with its obsidian reflections and
even the Aztecs who have taken
quarter on the south-side of legend
where the maize fields reach deep
into the prospect of another world
shadow figures of the many-gone
moving in shifts of pearl and
agate and the voices too high
above in a sky separated from
its own surface and the talking
going on beneath beds of leaf
and coral isn't it a wonder
you declaim in an archaic rhetoric
strictly speaking to blackboards
and the chalks of pure imagination
erecting libraries of untold verse

anemones of ocean and spittle
yards where unconfirmed children
spill over the little abysses shouts
that bring twilight to its knees
and the overt speculation about
madness and the splendors of weed
justice of the spoon and the horse
noontimes in the bedlam of memory
lunching with angels long dead
the massive cliffs overnight and
trumpets of vowel and diphthong
splitting the verger into unequal
hemispheres of bucolic and reverie
you keep making noises and rust
and its train of thought circling
mirrors of heat and the abacus
that lacks hands to count and
all the higher mathematics grown
red in the corner of the mind
that begins to see backwards into
the zero formulated by dying
just at the hour when moon and
steam conspire to shape the inks
of whatever it is that can be read
even as layers of silence mount
and wall and spool threaten
the remains of dust beautiful
spirals climbing pedestals of flame
into the depths of the galactic sea
the mind its portents of lasting
a longing to aspire to a dream
of the only thing that ever meant
to be the hand become inert
in its immense digital map
syntax and index of the finger
pointing to the maze of azure

air and its vanishing suburbs
fleeing forever into the past
you continue to declaim and
nothing ever comes back of that
passage through the underworld
asphodel blooms gone blind in
the inextinguishable lamp
rose and counter-rose paling
in the forever of an afterthought
has not been and what else
evening the fade of all

07-29-18

## TECHNIQUE OF OBLIVION

when the great year had come to a close
they took from us as a reward the thing
we loved most the dye not yet dry to grieve
which many agree is justice of the gods
the reluctance of light to share its shape
with the brief but catastrophic moment
when earth enters its shallow past a memento
of fading peninsulas and vertical horizons
the space to shift from a lunar cycle of heat
and the oscillating summers of sleep and
distances appropriate to rock and stone
to a circularity of mirrors and reflections
dimensions that touch the soul with a vertigo
and incandescence a solemnity of shadows
aching to return to their corporeal essence
wasn't that how we concluded the pact
with the deity who governs stairs and cigarettes
white situations that translate into leaf and
longing the ever decreasing pale of color
symptoms of a dying sun of a universe collapsed

**59**

on itself the spear-point of a chance vowel
separated from its meaning by syllables
of ink and sand delusional masks characters
drawn out of a despair to imitate music
never coming to the conclusive note sounding
iterations of brass and fog discrepancies
of minds adrift on nocturnal waters of absence
why did we not cry out to the passing stars
what was the instruction we so carefully followed
but misunderstood and the drowning voice
the calibration of hour and tempest the waves
lashing against the dissolving cliffs of our spirit
the poem never completed the shattered verse
if there really is another side to death one
which transposes breath and weight and size
into an enormous and luminous shape moving
mysteriously across the bay of memory
how will we ever know ?

07-31-18

*SPECULATIONS OF A SPHINX*

when the body separates from itself
where does the other body go
into what other night in time does
the escaping shadow evolve into
a still greater mystery without a past
when the soul is divided from itself
at the fatal moment when the moon
negates its lamp revolving around
an axis of heat and invisibility and
the immensity of the eye that dying
takes in all the remaining light
there is no more transparency
to air than there is to the circling sea

**60**

where memory emerged once shaking
off its pellucid skin in search of a
new shape an enigmatic voice
echoing the redundancies of rock
we stand on the other shore perplexed
watching the stone raft slowly
sink with its cargo of recollections
and final thoughts alone in our
abyss of misunderstanding and grief
the other body where is it going
sleep and the miasma of photons
a theogony of childhood puzzles
place names dissolved in a tumult
of syntax ink and tidal surges
the dream it was being this body
the formation of hands and the
eloquence of shoulders learning
to divine the cause for mourning
crying into the twilight grasses
searching for fingers and sashes
to tie around the senseless brain
to faint away and wake again
to the other day to the other dew
imaginations of a resurrection
in a world less new than the one
just abandoned not remembering
what had happened the night before
alarms and silences and rushing
of so many machines like gods
who have lost consciousness
in the long siege of oblivion
in the end what is there
but the empty cavity dust
people talking in the distance
making no sense of the event
earth in its infinite inch of loss

amazed that an enigma has taken
the body from the body

08-02-18

*SECRET MUSIC*

born without being asked permission
are distant from ourselves as mountains
dusky phantoms on the edge of reason
sea and cloud wharf and diamond-needle
sounding circles of midnight and aspirin
too soon misunderstood or negated lyric
the mind puzzled over the fracas of light
the leaves of sudden interpretation at
the window turning green the nocturne
that slowly instills the ear with a memory
whatever went before the accident the red
blooming artifice of words out of order
cannot be read will never say it right
tongue and maxillary a suggestion pale
as the already vanished dew the offering
of archaic instruments out of tune with
the stellar description notations in an ink
borrowed from a previous life the grieving
dawn after dawn of horses lost to the flame
where the house cannot be and going ever
towards a secret keep resonating with echoes
a stuff of the afterlife of hills and twilight
submerged worlds that could have been
had we not been born and the illusions
of skin and walking and the rock fragments
the polar inspections of nerve and diapason
mutilated glass mistaken for the spheres
revolving in their platonic ideation a full
moon about to implode the eye seeking

its other in the vague and enormous space
just outside the door the grass and ravines
sloping out towards the shell of existence
help was never on the way the radio turned
way up occlusions of vowel translations
of syllabic moments in the denial of time
wave length hours of the week it happened
the musicians in their scabbards oblivious
of the avenue of pure sunlight the reckoning
tensions of a movement marked adagio
shifting from tender rills into a pyramid
that cannot be counted like a coffin
inscribed with all the world's incantations
ash of sweetness then nothing the fading

08-03-18

*AWAKE BUT NOT AWAKE*

in a wheelbarrow they brought us
the remains of memory a pair of sleeves
some shoes without soles and buttonholes
overhead light rolled in waves like glass
in the field crickets were sewing a song
out of heat monotony and oblivion
it was the year without a face the month
called eternity and days like small cups
cracked and waiting on shelves of dust
the women who emerged from a myth
of trees and stone were heavy with names
like Daphne Persephone and Echo mirages
beautiful as a reminiscence of water in the hills
winds stopped to repair the chasm of noon
the sun with its enormous whetstone
seemed to be charged like an open wound
slowly removing its shadow from the sky

**63**

and voices of rock and sand like elves
that populate the ear of something dead
found by the side of the road resounded
incoherent with distance and longing
girls too without age pretty as amaryllis
growing in the crevices of earth approached
hands full of dirt clods & insect skeletons
chanting the miasma of an archaic trope
listening carefully to their rounded vowels
we ascertained nothing of their history
only the enormous and blank spaces
left behind by the syntax of moonlight
grief and mourning grass and shade
was there anything else to the Hour ?
we looked again into the wheelbarrow
smaller than we recalled hands folded
over his breast fragile as a hummingbird
sleeves shoes and buttonholes the remains
of memory a face emphasized by silence
and the hair as ever wonderfully unkempt

08-04-18



*AD INFINITUM*

at last the first a minute carved  out of space
and long now ashes gone to scatter in the air
a farewell a reminiscence from forty years ago
could nature be so indefinite as to winnow
from its winds a name a silhouette of sounds
circular and opaque and toss them far to sea
how comes now the dawn unrequited roses

**64**

stamped beneath the fiery hooves a lingering
of sparks and mornings that will never be
a freshet an eye of water a longing numbed
to the dissolved bone palest trace of matter
shade the former text revealing long stitches
lines unraveling between the hurried leaves
words snatched from a passing band of vowels
can never learn the tongue to speak aloud
or sing and mourn and grieve the error too
have lapsed again into senseless radiance
what breathed once now ashen emptiness

08-08-18

*THE DISAPPEARING SUMMER*

at the end of the road speaking Navajo or Chinese
they told us not to return to empty our luggage
out on the bed of withering leaves and weeds
the grassy relics of the dead we had borne
this far fearful of understanding their real nature
a past of secret longings intricacies and passions
of forbidden acts and rites committed behind
veils of stone and stained linens using knives
of vowel and myth a mystery of yearning inks
intended to hide the one thing they lacked
our dead the tender and sometimes cruel
revelations of light and contours like hills
arisen from pools of abandonment and shadow
what could we do standing there by trees
half undressed of their age the imperfect process
of distance climbing stubbornly the sun's late rays
into a month we could not enter a description
of memories without echo of a childhood
we had experienced together with our dead
or so we thought the mind being so numbed

**65**

by its own sleeping labyrinth of intricacy and doubt
whom could we ask to explain the immense air
and its writing in alphabets of aching winds
of rains predicted for their driving number and tone
syllables sounding like traces of honey on wax
dissolving in the dumb nocturne of a dream
that kept repeating itself in the nuance of color
spreading out above us as day waned into
a perpetuity of mountain and absence
the once unbearable heat now become a circle
of reminiscence a sand of disappearing monuments
our dead fingering their own ashes which we
tossed out to vistas of rugged and shapeless beauty
not given to understanding or explication
an edge of the world a motel of haunted ruin
a place to sleep the end of this tenuous summer
the lawn of sky flickering like a wet gutter
in the awesome portfolio of canyon and cliff
reddening in the terrible instant of recognition
ourselves and our dead side by side prepared
to disappear within the walls of echo

08-14-18


## THE DANCE OF IMMOBILITY

it wasn't just the hand that lacked gravity
but the plenitude and aura and print information
about thought and gyrating icons losing shape
and color and the insects at the barrier wanting in
the walls no longer visible the seas at the window
with their gravel of nocturnal longing and
passing by the phantom automobiles with their

wet tires sleek against the concrete leaving
behind traces of possible worlds of mountains
beneath the poetry of air and light and why go on
the body remained in its ineffable posture
as if asking questions no one could ever answer
expecting oracular lamps to shine on the enigma
enveloping the husk of breath swiftly departing
and what was there to say and listening carefully
to the weeping among the flowers without name
in the corridors and doors opening and closing
of their own and always the distant drone of a soul
testing its wings in an aleatory attempt at flight
whatever there was of weight and consequence
was of no moment now only the cracks in space
widening to let childhood out to vanish somewhere
in the greater horizon before time and grass and ink
the last yearning traces of an unremembered dream
invoked the elusive dance of immobility

08-16-18

*THE DANCE OF IMMOBILITY*

it wasn't just the hand that lacked gravity
but the plenitude and aura and print information
about thought and gyrating icons losing shape
and color and the insects at the barrier wanting in
the walls no longer visible the seas at the window
with their gravel of nocturnal longing and
passing by the phantom automobiles with their

wet tires sleek against the concrete leaving
behind traces of possible worlds of mountains
beneath the poetry of air and light and why go on
the body remained in its ineffable posture
as if asking questions no one could ever answer
expecting oracular lamps to shine on the enigma
enveloping the husk of breath swiftly departing
and what was there to say and listening carefully
to the weeping among the flowers without name
in the corridors and doors opening and closing
of their own and always the distant drone of a soul
testing its wings in an aleatory attempt at flight
whatever there was of weight and consequence
was of no moment now only the cracks in space
widening to let childhood out to vanish somewhere
in the greater horizon before time and grass and ink
the last yearning traces of an unremembered dream
invoked the elusive dance of immobility

08-16-18

## THE LAST GOODBYE

there is no recovered poem no access
to night no brightness around destiny
there is only the immense silence
that issues from beneath the door
from behind the x-ray or the date
circled in red on the discarded calendar
the months of ignoring the sun's

frequent disappearances behind
curtains of nebulous skies offer no
clues as to what happened when
the switch went off and the room
became immersed in a tenuous
gray film awash in millimeters
of an inexplicable rewinding of time
a tape recording or a mere sketch
of thought the going out into day
the underground path to the light
the unknown as always text hidden
somewhere in medical archives
or blotted out by mistake in a desk
filled with assorted and uncatalogued
data about the human condition
nothing really that can bear on
the missed possibilities or chances
was there ever an opportunity to
go back to return to some invisible
junction of months weeks days hours
was there ever a minute when life
itself could be reversed on its wheel
who could ever put the pieces back
locate the toys scattered on lawns
when twilight's longing distances
themselves become intransigent hills
that no one can climb or understand
a residency on earth punctuated
by the unexpected ambulance siren
or officials mute in their uniforms
looking on unable to speak because
a god has turned them to statues
and the lengthy irreversible walks
across gravel driveways that lead
either to a crematorium or a freeway
nothing ever prepares for the empty

ensuing prospects that extend
in all directions over a lost city
going to sleep but not sleeping
listening but not hearing voices
that transcend the dream of life
*far and away am I gone from you*

08-28-18


*MICRONAUT II*

the year more than half gone since you went
back into the invisible mountain to flower
again to renew the direction of your compass
to turn in your arms for elastic wings
more than half gone since you subtracted yourself
from the x-ray and the multiple prescriptions
from the puzzle of remaking yourself daily
attached to machines that recorded vital signs
what need had you of those artifacts anymore ?
the cosmos in a blink offered you the thrill
of flight interminable wonders of starry light
in all the hues imaginable and time itself
wound itself around the shape of your hand
and aloft you went cruising like a hummingbird
collecting the pollens of ecstasy and memory
inevitabilities of oblivion and space travel
such as you once imagined on Montague street
on a bicycle as if floating through clouds
over the demesne of the roiling bay waters
of the metropolis where you earned your life
as a pilot of plastic space-craft legitimacy
pivoting higher and higher over skyscrapers
and libraries the kite of your own fabrication
unraveling labyrinthine threads as you soared

master of the azure keeper of secret thunders
your eye on the fast winds that govern air
and the moon in its many phases where you
can land and observe distant earth revolving
far from the confusion it had once created when
your mind took a turn around the unexpected
+++++++++++++++++++++++++++++++++++++++++
more than six months now since you decided
yes the body is only weight and shadows can
be left behind to determine their own fates
you had learned and taught what you learned
to those too inept to figure it all out
you have become sleek a streaking flash
in the night heavens which we scour looking
for the brilliant dust of your swift passage
into eternity a micronaut at last

09-01-18

*THE WOUNDED SUN*

as much as it was a dream
                it really happened
his beautiful eyelashes – motionless
hands crossed over the still breast
a garland was made and a shroud to
cover his pale white face before being
delivered to the flames to be cleansed
a body no more but a mystery forever
a solitary traveler on the road
a shadow on the wane cast on gravel
or the rock abutments that mark
evening and the day's futile end
conclusions in clay and stone or
grass that ceases growing in its plot
window and door and sash shut tight

**71**

fingers left behind in the rushing
to and fro among those still living
a handsome figure in the photograph
a dreamy presumption of breath
clothes that no longer dress or fit
cold that seeps in under floorboards
and the stuttering light the phantom
lamp that hovers over the last hour
shedding its distant flare over walls
that keep nothing out but longing
the solitary stranger at the door
the thinly held mask the ribbons
fluttering in the breeze the fragment
of time chiseled out of the air
that bends its archaic self around
the leafless tree by the dry well
once held sacred to the goddess who
governs the shapes of sand and ink
who brings to bear on memory
the unbearable film of nostalgia
hills and islands and distant seas
where the wounded sun will go
to sleep in the spreading dark
*a body no more but a mystery forever*

09-03-18

## THE INEXPLICABLE

what is more random than an identity
a speck of dirt ashes star shards letters
not put together to form any meaning
bits and particles carried by the wind
blades of grass underfoot leaves heard
to whisper names from mythical times
water rushing through sleep unheard

dimensions of time and space reduced
to the size of a thumbnail the sorrowing
in the retold myth of Orpheus by his river
bled and carried his voice out to sea
singing in stone and tree and weeping
who can say how the shadow goes under
ground how arms raised to a black sun
suppliant and the slow revolutions of
the world on its wobbling axis and dark
the stilled inks of the many gone before
indiscernible masks personae unnamed
the chance germ that causes madness
and to not recognize and be seized by
and to render nil the small step forward
and to grace the breathing air of morning
with wan hope the distilled conscience
of the universe waking and not waking
in the mind's great probe to comprehend
it never was but a plaything of ideas
a sort of shorthand for the will to die
this everyday encounter with the void
we are not here we are not there
yet we stand unwittingly on cliff's edge
marveling at nature's massive beauty
cliffs conspiring to end all creation
in a single exultant crashing of silence
rock and cloud alike come thundering
through the sieve of light a catastrophe
no insurance can cover an ambulance
careening uncontrolled down city streets
bearing the sleight of hand formation
fever stricken shaking small cocoon
who never asked for and will never know
*why*

09-04-18

73

## THE HOSPITAL ROOM

antiseptic room whitewashed recall windows
left hanging in space yawning wide open on
the empty of it all the fade of vast the pale
sequences of air in knots vague solutions
pouring in the small porcelain sink a drone
humming machine cordless voices wafting
in the blanched noon of time running out
each is the inch of lost measures fever chart
diameters of the circles of heat illegible
in the rising mercury that records forgetting
steps taken back hands refolded critical
seconds counted backwards in the elevator
alphabetical conclusions voided red lining
zero effect nowhere to stare the walls passing
through limbo a hundred and more degrees
and raised into the ionosphere consciousness
ephemeral blinking lights a clasp broken
hemispheres that do not connect and here
the teratology of hieroglyph and abacus
the knocking metal in remembrance of lead
fission and break of a lunar landscape made
possible by fragments of light brought through
the refracted glass with its entropy scattering
in the aphasia of mid afternoon and nothing
to say or add to the report printed and handed
down to the subaltern in the last door to the left
corridors and wheels humans pushing carts
labeled with the detritus of the afterworld
how can we say these were the remaining
these were the minutes called to waste the hour
the effusion of fluorescence turning everything
into a hue of ennui a shading of impatience
worn like an apron around the doorkeeper

can we ever want to go back to that place
where oblivion takes hold of physical reality
numbing the crevices and falling silences
cannot echo the least cipher failing the thermometer
telephone call of rapid ingots misunderstanding
the rupture meant of words in recoil
absence of nerve a shape looming like
ink clouds everything talking into a switch
levers of history lifting the unwritten into
a code of sweating sheets the face turned
away from the empyrean of memory a shift
in weight a sudden loss of gravity the drop
of colorless liquid that absorbs the cosmos
*ting ting ting* the tiniest nuance of sound
that drains the ear of all rumor x-ray
of noise diminished in the whitening whole
until sad the lost and longing fingers
can no more hang on to the fraying air
the room resumes its prehistoric shape
glacial remote as the first day of space

09-05-18

## THE MATERIAL WORLD

and what if you know these things some
of these things and it hurts you so the
grieving over these things the rainfall
and mist and duplicity of light and lies
about what you do and do not know
like the cycles of heat and radiation
or the way gathering some of these things

**75**

to throw them away is a decision you
cannot make and it does hurt to recall
the use of these things the deviant shade
cast upon them the alley and the grove
trees and the big hedge around the yard
to hurt the sun to cut deep into its core
you tried and scant was the learning
to throw the spear or wield the two-
edged weapon what was it called these
matters always at the bottom of it the
language or its lack the echo but not
the silence gathered like a knot around
it the dolorous movement between and
in and out of these things to have knowledge and the capacity for tears shoulders
do and weep in the hidden hours of night
by whose bedside and by whose shadow
you will begin to know but never completely
the formation of matter the growth of
rock crystal the moon for example in its
first budding and the red the intensity
of red in the history that governs time
are you thinking something else or a hand
a lifted ornament a shining in the fingers
a clasp in the dark a shudder lightning
at the window as if asking to come in
to be seated beside the now many ghosts
parallels to thinking they are in the next
life by now looking back at us so you
imagine a theater to be crowded in ex-
pectation of a punctuation that will render
the soul releasing it from the broken cage
the ribs that hold fast to song these small
things cannot be enumerated in sleep
where dreaming there is an exit from
matter a way out of the labyrinthine puzzle

where we are looking around at how much
we have collected and you wonder at
the price that it has fallen and no one
really cares fingering old photos yellow
with age the so called devastation of hours
eating away at the recollection of it all
you are going to start weeping again it
can't be helped so much like a flood of
shattered light transept and key and map
unfolded knees trembling cannot have it
back can no more call them your own
these things by which you thought life
was defined it was really in the little
hands of aphasia the blocked passage
to memory the vowels iterated but misunderstood could not make sense of it
coming back from the mortuary after
the cleansing by fire watching the signs
go the other way the traffic bearing these
things to the other world of silence
and longing the swift passing of every
       *thing*

09-09-18


## THE SOUL'S FIRST HALF YEAR OF ETERNITY

what follows the interruption of memory ?
what is the collateral damage of thought ?
where in the world does *it* go ? ashes up
the chimney clouds billowing senselessly
across the small patch of remaining summer
fingers wasted in their grassy search
for the body's short lived outline

the whole subtracted from the half !
where is the hemisphere of occlusions ?
flowers distances longings fractures
the list of nominals darkens in the ascent
to heaven or so say the entomologists
who have spent their day carving sand
into images of light and space the immense
that whitens the deeper sleep loses its
borders entering the unending realm
the soul the fleeting fragile winged thing
puzzled at the loss of recognition
of recollections that no longer make sense
espying in the lessening globe below
a turbulence of water and voices like
ropes frayed by lesions of invisibility
what winds ! how many inches left of time ?
does it ever come back the dream of *being* ?
isolation and the diminishing scales of weight
gravity itself the speck of red in the upper
left quadrant of a map maker's amnesia
nothing and less than nothing the rooms
emptied of the anesthesia of language
what use is it to go back and look ?
someone during the night has processed
the dust replacing the hills with twilight
here and here and here there were
rocks markers on the way home
where are they now ?

09-16-18

## THE CHILDREN'S HOUR

the kingdom of the sun with its glistening & errant
cattle and the hives and caves and crypts secrets
great and wide beneath the endless awning sky
of a single afternoon and the famous grass
and the continents that swarm beneath an eyelid
dreaming countries of ink and saffron sands
heights of splendid but drowsy towers the paths
that lead inwards in the grotto of miscomprehension
tinsel and toys and spectra of the dissonance of red
champions fused to their steeds tilting with ether
or clots of blood the unexpected emergency bell
sounding off the brain taken by make-believe
will never be hours such as were in the afterthought
barons and kings of petty isles and refrains silver
as the distance of the moon and twilight setting in
with hills of stars and mannequins talking big
their vowels and consonants sparkling in the dark
but the mind ! the language of sleep with its
multiple psyche and the forbidden gates of time
an echo resounding through all the eons of rock
the *Library* in the midst of such an alphabetic din
where crouching in a daft innocence children
take on their phantom doubles and increase
though sick to the death an ineffable wisdom
shale and tufa and sandstone lions dissolving
like mists in the smoking curtain of the Hesperides
was here and here alone the signal manifested
and x-rays and portents of space travel and magnets
that draw words backwards through their embryos
to make of speech a transfer of stone and leaf
visions only possible through hieroglyphic error
asterisks of tongue and long and silent sequences
embroidered by a crazy quilt of remembered hands

to hold and let go and fly into an absent heaven
where the magic Hour extends its minute forever

09-20-18

*THE PRISON OF LIGHT*

it didn't take long and the grass mowed
and the weeds neatly dispatched by twilight
browning hedges eclipses of the moon
seen only by the left eye a total surrender
to the shoulder gifted with weeping and
to the surprise of the gravel path the garden
in disarray the emotions of budding daisies
tender disregard of the hollyhocks swaying
in the collapsed wind what was one to make
of the signal red of despair echoing wildly
among dizzying swarms of bees intent on
bringing amazement to the mantle of sorrow
that embraced the western hills the burgeoning
apses in the secret location of the stop-watch
sandy shifts of sleep the slow herds shaggy
dreaming tender as night inside the rock
the perforated air & the mourning cascade
echelons of unuttered vowels bright in the ear
dormant cliffs steeped into the mind's lair
cold abutment of reason unwired gone lost
fragments of stone formations and seas
swirling with oracular echoes surf shots
of dissonance chaos of beauty in its embryo
how much longing in the stamen and pistil
the blind roots whitening with sorrowed
absence in search of an earth below the earth
mythic voices from the depths of time
syllables the shape of inverted pyramids
a music that goes out like a rope dissolved

**80**

by infinite salts and the vast empyrean itself
flung like a senseless arm into far reaches
where the soul released from the prison of light
wanders weightless free of all absurdities

09-22-18


*MAX TRANSFORMED*

I saw it despite the rock escarpment
at the foot of the bed the shadowy flute player
and the big Buddha who governs attachment
and the length of time each nodding off to sleep
and when the electrical monument shuddered
momentarily bringing darkness to the walls
I felt something enter my arm and travel
like lightning through my veins and from a cavern
far to the south of here a voice indistinct at first
came through the glass asking for mother
it was the echo of memory talking without vowels
smooth utterances of cooing like doves in the attic
where they distill thoughts and scatter them
like pollen in the morning winds before dawn
has a chance to spell out the shapes of light
already something else was working in my ear
a mountain mysterious as the weight of ink
or nothing more than some sand loosened
from a statue that was not able to stand
because it had not been granted breath and tottered
massive shifts of space and planets out of orbit
and the form of gravity like a shoe that
remained untied and the foot and the hand and
the nerve that controls whatever it is the eye beholds
I took all of these as signs that childhood

had come to an end and that something new
enormous with silence and untapped energies
was going to emerge from that small place where
people cry unable to understand that there is nothing
to understand and then without feeling it
the great transformation commenced with its toys
beyond touch and the hair uncombed and
whatever else it takes to resemble a body
which is no more than a lapse of memory
an invisible wriggling of the impulse to sleep
the sleep which is the forever of an uncounted moment
took me softly from those whose doorways
half shut darkened and their fingers and

09-22-18


*CLIMBING THE LIGHT*

disobliged by sorrow at the excavations
you kept picking and digging looking
for the city that was your birthright
walls and urns and shattered echoes
gold effluvia the content of archaic air
could not wait for the clarion to summon
phantoms of mountain and dust to appear
dawn's chariot still darkened at the gate
your bed left undone your body gone
how was the soul to flee from these ruins
one layer of history at a time destroyed
ten deep the antiquities of Chaos !
cease writing ! everything has turned to marble
the birds of the air the fish in the ponds
to move even a finger is a matter of weight
the inks have dried on the parchment
red has replaced black in the lunations

no one is waiting for you at the portal
the anesthetician has mistaken you for
the mask being fitted over the memory
of the *other* who arrives tomorrow
signatures and feathers and asterisks
empty of meaning are gathered for auction
outside the once great portico on the hill
will you ever be able to come back
to claim your shadow and silhouette ?

09-25-18

*WHAT IS THERE TO FORGET ?*

when you got to the other bank
was the alphabet of the fire still legible ?
were the hands that illustrated you once
now the shapes of smoke and illusion ?
how many were the waters between this side
and the other that ferried you over ?
when you reached the opposite shore
what was left of the memory of this one
where we reside waiting for an impossibility ?
two times two will never be the same again
stone and grass and the long stretches of sky
that glide serenely between the termini
the one of being born the other of going away
how can we account for the day of the accident ?
what was the semaphore in the air flashing
that no one could notice it and the sound
of the ampersand and the wailing asterisk
and the furious decibels beyond hearing
which of us could understand that in the doorway
mystery was assuming the weight of ink
shadows from the other bank beckoned
echoes of a language that employs silence

**83**

as an exclamation mark and vowels
that run their course in a single flute note
tell us then that in that other distance
where your remains have become heat cycles
vertiginous summers in the dust bin of time
small ciphers of a quantum physics
that extends itself into the noon of statues
you somehow continue to exist a recollection
of flight without wings of heights without motion
and whenever the word *love* is mentioned
the mourning dove emits its ineffable cry
and the wind shakes all the leaves
still shining in the air
what is there to forget ?

09-28-18


## CHILD-OF-MY-HEART

which was the hieroglyph that interpreted you ?
was it the leaf learning to read the light
and what it has to say descending on its ladder
of invisible floral patterns and moon thoughts ?
you reached out for a handful of air
to define your true being the essential inner you
great internal blossoming of sand and rock
imprinted with the hearsay of the archaic
enormous unfolding waves of letters
missives from secret gods hidden in liquid gold
what their mouths were telling you in a language
of fever and ancient fingerprints HOIL
which you wrote in your mysterious passage
to the underworld riding the enigmatic thunder
deep into the recesses far beyond the cathode ray
where lightning bugs and fairy princes toiled

**84**

to remove the blister from the mind
intelligence of a higher order spatial careening
within the thumb and its aureole you held aloft
staring at times for an eon into the miasma
and corolla of the bedside plant emerging
from the souls of the Philipino or Nigerian nurses
who helped you turn from one hemisphere to the other
blazing ingots of midnight spheres swirling
in the forever of your crabbed Egyptian handwriting
Child-of-my-Heart ! how could I know that to
pick you up and address your frail weight
was an error a millimeter of breath and truth
misunderstanding of the hundred thousand isotopes
that converged to remove your body from its
burning and naked shadow the one and the two
that summed you up between the galaxies
that were either coming to a sublime end
or that were just being born again

10-02-18

## WEDNESDAY FOREVER

flowers that make a week
Februaries that make a day
time passing and all the time that will
not pass again and the showers from clouds
of a single Wednesday with its hidden continents
its errors of passage and deliberation
a crown of grief a salient stanza in a poem
with bodies of rain and intricacies of wind
that wrap around the trunk of a lone tree
still-born memories in the leafless branches
a voice of air laced with tomorrow's dewfall
a night that is no night at all but the whole
of space before the echo of light

**85**

the long erroneous river of cold flame
wending its way through stubborn rock
sands and unmitigated shores no step has moved
and isolated bunches of thought gathered
in a simple vowel resonating in a canyon
somewhere to the far west of the unspoken line
margins fluid and open to interpretation
inks of hieroglyphs yet to be discovered
underneath the clinical stone of speech
number itself the zero in residence of waters
rushing through the one ear of sleep
and nothing but paper waste the sadness
of trying over and over to understand the why
of being born the what of coming to be
grass and evening and heights vanishing
as all distances do in the eye's incapacity
to perceive whether it is a mountain or
the oncoming darkness that takes us by the knees
wavering as we approach the mystery
unfolding in the labyrinthine and plural sky
*why did we not recognize it for the ending*
                              *that it was ?*

10-03-18


## THE GOING FORTH

it's easy to lose balance to fall from the light
displace the body from its wandering shadow
lift three fingers instead of five of a hand
that is already bound the other way to death's
fixed abode on the margins of space you know
where the radio and the ice-box and the car
cease functioning and then to try to pick yourself up

**86**

forgetting that the world is best seen upside down
the medical units of sound the sirens of eerie silence
those who address the gods as an attribute or
routine of cloud formation and to drive the syntax
of oblivion on to the runway and watch it take
flight and abandon the beautiful license plates
to be enumerated and isn't the next day of death
really the first among many that lack the number
zero and aleph and zed and multiply it all with
a glove that fits over the missing hand and let sleep
and its oneiric frigate into the lethal waters the
overpowering sensation of falling in love even as
the body is lifted from its wrack by an engine
of floss and hair and someone else whispers into
the remaining ear that drains the air of honey
and wounds manifest and misunderstanding of
the genesis of things like bees in their hive of
madness to know at a speed that reddens sky
the enormous ellipse in that falling the immediate
shock of wisdom come too late the broken bones
cerebral flashes of *inwit* that burn to the marrow
how will this take place tomorrow ? which is the
one if not the two of pure identity ? *you* are the mask
the unknown to the other the person unredeemed
waiting for a sort of rebirth a Pythagorean bean-field
to be picked and swallowed and inured to breath
numbing sensation of *déjà vu* even as you try to
reassemble the parts ignoring the fact that you
do not know which parts go where and the aliens
buzzing around you with machines and beepers and
stretchers and other ontological paraphernalia
it is all a failed network of lexicography a syllable
that cannot be pronounced right a vowel caught high
in the dark that proceeds slowly from the mind

10-03-18

*SHORT CIRCUIT*
        *for Marilla*

I can't tie my shoe strings
my pulse is fluttering madly
black spots devour my left eye
and people randomly assembled
all with someone else's hands
what are they doing and saying
where is the illuminated globe
and the scissors that cut the wind
and leaves that are the real
forms of speech and lamenting
if I lean over earth flies up
and hits me in the face a shock
to have been born they say
to knots of air and lungs like
bellows working over time
hours in the place where it hurts
no limit to the lack of focus
grass nibbling the edges of ink
and to be sure an angel hovering
the weight of a single rain drop
is it because half the light is gone
that futures of stone and sand
have been cancelled in flight
clouds and the tops of trees
make the horizon of what I see
sometimes a paper boat in the tub
or a kite released from my fingers
floating like painted dream
in the farthest reaches of sky
otherwise night has its surface
spreading over my distant feet

**88**

and the language of ether and myth
indecipherable syllables flood
the wreckage of what I can hear
listing vowels and the sweet flute
of an organized religion sings
mother comes back from lunch
and together we recite the bed
sheets and crowns of liquid hair
is it possible to ever recall why
the engine short circuited ?

10-04-18

*STELLA MARIS*

last time he's ever going to sleep
and with a high fever
        won't wake up any more
petals floating down on glass
white on white translucent
            the swan traced in its sky of ivory
of going across the sea to the love Unknown
        can't arouse him any more
like the time we walked and walked him
round the neighborhood looking at all the trees
            leaves firm in their decision to sleep
ash shaken from crystal / heat born in cycles
the hand gone from its shape / shadow no more
            heights and precipices
what was the heresy and what was the cure
to headlands gone the horses swift and black
            the one named Ariel the other nameless
look deep into his eyes for the remains
                pools of light and all they contain
weeping at the sound and the barge
come to the limits of water and stone

**89**

strophes counted in fahrenheit
image of angels hewn from basalt
shining and not shining in the afterwards
in what unnamed wood proceeding
the soul or whatever be its denomination
climbing one by one the piers of flame
& in the empyrean are etched the stars
turned green in the maze / the hidden leaf
design and focus of the sun / coffin of light
clings to air nothing / ether
when the window turned and the bridge
the guiding principle of distance
in the sulfurous sunset
glow of after-things of what cannot be
named or otherwise
among animals and Christians
unable to count past fifty / misunderstand salvation
devotion to *Stella Maris*
and we are among the lower order
the ones who cannot wake properly
in a bed of straw and shivering
the planet Nemesis hove into view
for three weeks in January did not "connect"
the eye / *lachrymae rerum*
and what they call the moon when it becomes
invisible / the phantom Helen
and are come to naught the many
appeals to the Olympians
white-armed Juno *angry*
destroyed most the fleet / haze
miasma of the noontime seas / sensation
of drowning / how could such an episode
not spell the end ?

10-05-18

## THE UNPERCEIVED MYSTERY

what is illustrated by the small cry
in the midst of sleep the incoherence
of the skies as they draw to a close
the fixed and former planets now dust
ineffable losses of formation and weight
where speech no longer works and silence
is an inexpressible ingot of absent syllables
who will be the first to lift the hand of thought
to resuscitate the contours of syntax in
the vain effort to reorganize memory
what collapses repeatedly is the center
the oval ellipse of a noon without statues
climbing the steep western slope of amnesia
mistaking for persons the illusory masks
that stare out of shop windows wondering
whether there will be sufficient light
to carry on for the day's lost remainder
such as it is we wake and wash and walk
opening doors shutting latches blinking
like animals new to the phosphorescence
of a world filled with mistaken confirmations
a tree beside its rock of consciousness
some water that turns air into indecision
clouds lapsed into a coma of lost summers
heights ! dreams suddenly return their ink
etched in the Mediterranean brilliance
the sun casts its long shadow of sands
we listen for the echo inherent in leaves
turning to one another deaf to the vowel
that informs the winds of the mystery
being alive succumbing to breath dying

10-07-18

## IN PERPETUITY

all the schools of thought
fit into a single blade of grass
the heat and magma of the past
the very turbulence of the cosmos
a dew drop a petal in the wind
all expressions of the seen and felt
are nothing in the sweep of time
a second ago when the play of nerve
and finger seemed like music
shaped and sensed by the mind
now a spot of ash an incinerated thought
come down to earth the rapacious gods
flash their gaudy crowns
parading magnificent see-through
bodies like shadows of alabaster
they too are nothing but absence
of matter eloquence of empty space
the unspeakable chastity of air
rewinding the myth of circularity
stars and their awesome punctuation
that flood the night in a single blink
leave not a trace of the vast Unknown
how do we then speak pronouncing
lives that have occurred in
the passing vowel pure sound
echo of an echo buried in stone
what can we say to the gone one
whose sad distance is now a sleep
a phrase of darkness and fading
how can we say to him *come back*
the book of lawns is empty
kites no longer page the heavens
each step through murmurs

whispered in the leaves erased
a voice of silence what else remains
in perpetuity

10-09-18


## THE SECRET MAX

full as the light of day he was
and from either hemisphere took
the shining bright as islands afloat
in the noon time seas he was a presence
all around a center and two margins
a north and south the flight of unseen things
his eyes if not the sky that flooded them
the moon and clouds like gossamer
passing through worlds of glass illusion
a lawn a backyard roofs and windows
an entire house of summers and trees
that made of everything a secret of shadow
and basement stairs and mornings too
come sudden as lamps from antiquity
talking statues pedestals and large vases
painted with the likeness of the other time
great was the sun and phrases like horses
hauling invisible poles and barges of stars
to listen and feel the curvature of time
the gravity of space lost by a single inch
intrepid as hair uncombed and smiles
the size of wounded inks a story to remain
untold a verse never polished the unfinished
wheel and the chairs all around solemn
to begin crying because the rug or a wall
what was out of place he wasn't there
anymore the sign of souls that take wing

**93**

the last he was to mark the record
with his passing fingertip and thumbs
and feet like angels that don't exist
was here and not here the day he filled
and grass and loss and longing paths
wherever to look and blind to see

10-09-18

*ZERO !*

into which hemisphere of light did he disappear ?
did the god of invisible trees take him ?
in the section of space where there is no sky
where the bodies of *Echo* migrate is there
a blade of grass where his memory rests ?
into what river that does not exist did he step ?
or did he simply slip into the chasm of air and ink
from which there is no return to day ?
to speak of emptiness does not suffice
nor to grieve overmuch the missing finger
lost in the Sargasso lawns of twilight
nothing explains the minute when everything occurs
yet nothing has ever happened
but the opening up of winds that mourn
their loss of shape and embodiment of voice
waters ethers earths voids of fire and ice
fevers mount on the sliver of mind
x-rays detonate the few sounds that remain
indelible vowels of eternity
how was it that when we turned our backs
a shadow of intricate subtractions deprived us
of sight and hearing both ? *Zero !*
did we not perceive new wings taking flight ?
a sun of archaic stone radiates its silence
over the inexplicable mystery

**94**

that leaves us on this side of death
hemispheres of light ! bodies of *Echo !*

10-11-18

*THE MORGUE*

what joy to speak the languages of my youth
to spout poetry in all those romance dialects
to embrace and be embraced by *Jaufre Rudel*
and sing *"Lanquan li jorn son lonc en may"*
and yet and yet I am haunted by those days
in the morgue the cold unconscious sun
lying there rising setting rising setting no
more the empty of the center of the seed
blackening at the root frigid at the core
seams undone rays that once spread through
all of space and short of the day's last mark
the punctuation of voice and bright hair stilled
nor by the wind undone nor by comb seized
brow and knee and fuse of fingers to the bone
nor by grass tickled the inorganic mass quiet
decomposing an anthology of senses blotted
out by some savage ink and not even to sit up
be counted erase conjectures shout to the sleepers
it's come to be what never was the now silent
and gelid zoom of time's relentless bit make inert
the once vivid light-filled boy the leaping counter
to gravity and the spackled room of stars alas
what do the literati say the faceless teachers
whose job is to gather from the planetary dark
some relics what few scraps to remember worthy
of what was thought and said sometimes written
down turned to verse or liturgy mosaic or melody
but in the morgue immobility and lack of sound
the distance of melancholy meters blanked out

**95**

footsteps and falling petals ocher bleached
landscapes of forever fade the pale vast void
untouched and untouchable the gone I cannot
get out of mind not the pure nostalgia of the
first modern poet *Jaufre Rudel* but antinomies
of matter and truly senseless decay sadness
the shut door the lock and latch and missing key
this the basement that terrified the puzzled child
the bottomless sequence of ladders and traps
the hole from which no hand returns the depth
and ancient well where they hide the moons
*red* no more but the color of cast iron and anvils
Pluto's sheer white madness of beyond the pale
and then what ? and then what ? lying there
whom I cannot exorcise from mind but sleep
alone in the frozen bed unaccompanied by the Lark
by the Primavera whose nimble feet danced on air
and waters and sands and pallid pink shells once
to birth gave consciousness and the Master Sun
not even a whisper in the labyrinthine whorls
the ear once a frieze of echoes now impenetrable
what was once my son the end of time

10-11-18

*FATE*

when they wrote that page
who was at the window watching ?
who could restrain the hands of the wind ?
it came from a chasm of ink
illegible words of a rotating night
errors in punctuation and syntax
what could be the one way forward
if not opening the side door
and going directly into the woods

it was the century after Dante
harmonies of otherworldly voices
and an afternoon of sublime intonations
that page they had written
when did it disappear from view ?
we went to the mountain and asked
we dropped pebbles into a white urn
and listened for the river at the bottom
without an answer we returned home
only to find the tree uprooted
the wall broken in half at the north
an ambulance had just arrived
to bear the illness away to its secret
how many years in a small thimble ?
prayer and illusion and signatures
what else was there to undress ?
the consulted oracle gave us a few vowels
a signal that blinked at odd hours
numerals to be deciphered in sleep
a dream of immense clouds
that meant absolutely nothing
such weathers and atmospheres were life
itself the indeterminate forms
of the soul trapped in a rib cage
had we only paid attention to the page
at the beginning of the hour
and who was at the window watching
instead we worried about combs
about wax and keys and storefronts
the ambulance came back forth
how many times ? an echo
from insurmountable distances
the unrestrained wind
chasm of ink

10-15-18

*THE FATED ONE*

half illusion half hemisphere
the part of life now slipped into cloud
silent music of sand and grains of amethyst
hands still talking to their absent shapes
a mirror in reverse and heights so dizzy
all names recede for fear of falling
a Japanese fan over a non-existent pool
in which reflections of souls for a minute
assume bodies of invisible black suns
then vanish like continents of dew
into the outer hemisphere of light
the illusory half that never was
but a sea divided into synchronicities
of Nymph and daffodil still comatose
in the arm of Morpheus in his fog
rosary of pearls and memories
swift walking shadows on the rim of time
a dozen acolytes of Dawn entranced
among the sleepers who cleave to ink
phosphorous of mind the *fated* one
charged with enigmatic flame set forth
foot knee hip and shoulder illumined
to tread earth's dusky monograph
just once before by chaos embraced
and returned to echo's twilight vowel
mystery of uneven halves
the unknown whole
that slipped away

10-16-18

## THOUSANDS OF YEARS

two things thousands of years old
in my mind one is my dead son
the other my dead brother
both like unseen planets
circling in the black solar hour
when the bridge of words fails
to convey these massive stone fragments
                    *Olmec* heads
to their place of silence and solitude
thousands of years old yet weightless
plunging into the jade pool of oblivion
one is a humming bird the other a flute
porous rock the sky promised to them
millennial ivy darkening on the stucco wall
will hold them for the brief instant of infinity
light from another source a blaze of fireflies
will illumine their immense but empty forms
grasses and jungle saliva and depths of space
their unknown and final destination
thousands of years in the making
thousands of years in my mind fluttering
like dusty wings of moth or butterfly
long gone into the summer pageant
of distance and echo
*thousands of years*

10-18-18

**99**

## MAGIC MAX

tell me you've just gone
to a temporary Elysium
where flowers are made of paper
in colors that last a day
a place where they burn water
because death does not exist
tell me that on the other shore
your hands are still making
shadows that the blind can feel
that instead of night a sort
of river runs through the mind
bearing candles just gone out
tell me memory is but a game
invented by the gods who
set up rocks and mountains
where nothing was before
a world where triangles sound
between vast silences of time
and the distance between
sleep and the tomb of light
is that brief inch of chaos
where your last x-ray stands
permanently on display
tell me that tomorrow
after years of concentration
you'll be on your way back
that the cardboard box
where they put your hair
and the business envelope
where medical records fester
have been tossed into the ditch
that echoes of what you thought
and words you could never say

are engraved on red litmus
to shine throughout the *Hour*
tell me please it won't be long
before each vowel and consonant
of your beautiful aphasia
will be pronounced an oracle
tell me something besides
the darkness that riddles space
that your small afternoon
of bright smoke was a dream
a recording from a different life
a semblance of the body
you left far behind
in the temporary Elysium
somewhere beyond the sun
that you'll be home tomorrow
to test our love and say
you never went away

10-21-18

## THE LAST WEDNESDAY

who lives behind the Sound ? the echo
dwelling in the ear maze and portico
of memories now dimming without light
what were they trying to tell us that morning
fateful whispers hints of walls of incompletion
the sundered hand the frenzied glance of breath
illegible yet with all clarity death's admonition
how incomparable the morning's strange glow
the flowing under of the undetected stream
stygian darkness rippling waters without gravity
a moon ascending in the mid-day hour its eye
whiter than the dazed shape of the letter zed
and the geese ! shaping a cuneiform flight

**101**

into a heaven unblemished by neon or mercury
wavering absences of all we should have known
great lifted weights tombstones of memory
the small incisions lesser spatial wounds
still we balanced inaction against its spirals
exchanging notes with the sad physician
what was to understand if not the flowers
beckoning us outside to memorialize regret
functions of the tongue uttering unthought words
dreaming green eclipses that dozing planets
curve in their fatal plunge through ozone
into Vishnu's wading pond the end of time
in circumscribed dots a stellar punctuation
gone awry to understand the what the why and
tragic curlicues that emphasize the gone
what were they telling us in that archaic code
oracular misspellings rotating devices winds
that lessened their immense inks beating
tiny hands against now darkened windows
look again into those eyes pleading to let go
*be free !* hummingbird winging silently
into the deep Unknown

10-24-18

*THE IRREVOCABLE*

I am gone it says the body
the corrupt self waiting at the counter
all these years for an intaglio of light
a metal object in the sky
the divided half of the half
swooning before the language of rushes
at the border before becoming crimson
a sun nearly disappeared in its faint
commas and aspersions of the moon

**102**

if it sets tonight and what will
it have cost us to say why
the reply hidden in the envelope
with the cut hair like grass not fresh
a voice coming from the Trojan women
or on the turret with the boy
eye on the passing cloud frame
hands no longer attached to the
whole exactly when the bell rings
the lunge against the race feet
of dust and the long shoreline solitude
when did we ever it asks in dark
tones the woods as if receding
memory the quiet valve being turned
off the definition of person
a pronoun in search of a mask
it is huge out there the origins of space
continents of gas whirling around
the small imprecision of number
perfection does not become mortals
nor flight which is left to gods
the abstract and the revolving
come to shadows and walking
as if in a trance the soul
require of it nothing a
blossom or a firefly in extent of
breath and writing

10-25-18

## MEDITATION

not a day passes when I do not meditate
on my poor son's death the before and after
of the alphabet the string of hours in a drop of dew
the echo which does not have a sound to generate
not a day passes when I do not call out in vain his name
unorganized space the void of penalty and default
the city built upon ten others destroyed within a day
the passage of gods who govern nothing more than hair
and combs and lovely necklaces of human skull
that I do not meditate on the flimsy fabric of light
the origins of gravity and loss and puerile fantasies
of poetry written in a single night to describe
the epos of birth and endless dying in love and ink
swarms of bees covering the air with buzzing script
and ants and other tiny winged things that excavate
what the mind does never think the vast and empty
of everything that has ever been and flowers and wells
and drinking spoons the thimbles of circular ideas
heat that passes like invisible bodies in summers of despair
and logic and circumcision and poverties of religion
books in fact I can never read wherein is defined
what dying is to stone and memory and rock formations
in the midst of clouds and the failing punctuations
of oracular declamation the enigma pronounced as if
silence were the audience in a world of decaying sand
a life it was I tell myself a meditation of coils and time
threading through elaborate mounds of wind and silk
an afternoon spent in windows that do not reflect
and jewels stolen in the maze of sounds the round
of masks dancing on a single hand and what's more
to meditate than that when I think of his dying last
the impossibility of leaves that talk dreaming sleep
will be the only thing remembered in the past

10-26-18

*CHRYSANTHEMUMS*
  *for Marilla, our 56ᵗʰ anniversary*

locked illusions of streets run wild
the famous illiteracy of the park
when dusk takes an oath to never
move the hills of yearning distance
nor of the river that fades green
in the elliptic awning of the years
champion in the bushes tilts with
stippled rays of light the high and ho
in archaic late medieval Spanish
to capture in all its essence love's
monthly magazine of gloss and wing
*she is the was the my-ever-will-be*
on a raft of silver celluloid floating
derelict in post-adolescent heaven
beside the flying fish of ancient south
deathless swoon resolved by night
'ere flinging stars their cadavers glow
a flame a single spark the wedding vow
epithalamium in cinematic flashback
the entire cycle of romance philology
chrysanthemums full blown rich golden
hues that decorate mountains of the mind
come forth the yellows equal to an ocher
bled into orange bridges spanning fast
waters of swirling palmistry and lore
doves aloft spun out of control soaring
like clouds and India ink and chalks
writing through the dream a reverie
to last a lifetime and undergo buffets
destroying coastlines the unendurable
toss of fate to go either way into dark

**105**

surviving *that* the opposite shore erects
a cliff sown with mums and setting suns
a-flare in autumnal melancholy brass
the ear flooding with sad horns and
tender finalities the whispered end
of what we share enigmatic
and forever the Unknown

10-27-18


## THE REMAINS

the discarded comb
the useless shaving brush
and what the mirror no longer holds
distance of immeasurable hours
nowhere now in the spent landscape
of discarded talismans the photo X
the door which is only a reversal
of the outside of things vertigo
and drumroll and silence wherever
feet used to attempt an escape
or arms in sleeveless ambition to rise
lifting from the ponies of gravity
a body surfeit of bone and thought
small shadows of memory
lingering in unlit passageways
listening for the call-bell
the minute issue of aphasia
in the dissembled space of night
the known and the unknown balled
up in a fist of courage to move
only to stop on the vowel
capable of igniting the last flame

**106**

a section of air the rebuttal of breath
winnowing clouds with a single finger
the shoelace and the device
which lacks a name and now lies
like a subsidiary to rust somewhere
by the window looking west
the area of empty garages and
wheels turning slowly without
direction and everything else
that used to function for reasons
that never could be explained

10-28-18

*THE BELL TOLLS FOR THEE*

the man on the cross
does not with light
pierced his body
return this night
of all days the least
bright the lesser
hour the briefest
breath any moment
to go out at last

as stars their infinite
route nothing determine
of man's fate
so all Tuedays
in perpetual gyration
add to the wheel of numbers
nothing but despair's
zero formation

when the last was caught

and still alive shifting
between all hues of Iris
who flitting unshod
from cloud to cloud
brings only messages
of ill augur to dreams
and waking knows
not another day of
light will be his
infirm of heat and
breathless

slowly the unwinding
hour the lessened sand
sifting through narrows
of language and thought
'til silence is the all
the fixed signal of
ending a hand and
its outline the shadow
of what once moved
in its grasp the null
and void of eternity

will weep the descent
underground white
writhing the roots
that cling to hope
as the body removed
from its cross and
washed and scraped
of error and sublime
flame awaits its
last the journey out
kempt and trimmed
transfigured memory

how air is great
in billows of rolling
blank summers once
the greenery of life
rivers and running
between pyramids of
shadow and grass
sutures of air unseen
the wounded soul
struggling for its
release the only
whispering echoes
of was

the bell and drum
the castanets whatever
else makes sound
in the small shell
distances of seas
roaring afflicted
and darkness rolling
waves across
the spatial void

*him remember who*
*joy to your life*
*brought*

10-30-18

*ANIMULA VAGULA BLANDULA*

the soul what is it often we ask
invented by the Ionian Greeks but
when it enters cloud speaks Persian

**109**

looking for the park called paradise
as far east as Japanese it speaks
either with or without wings and
compared to hummingbird or butterfly
is probably less mobile than stone
when it comes to sleeping and other
distinctions include ethereal doped
on atmospheres of sublimity and
awkward when it comes to stairs
or smoke and iridescent in sunlight
opaque as ocean in moonlight and
seen sobbing by fallen trees or
without raiment it seems to have
the outlines of body or shadow
or something even more primordial
circular in fact and ideational
as to content and the purpose of
flight and its opposite falling
ceaselessly through thought indigo
and vermillion and azure like liquid
which has yet to be distilled in glass
seen from the other side it appears to
levitate like gasoline on a hot day
off the pavement of an isolated highway
then it enters canyons to wash itself
of memory to return dazed a fragment
of wind or space and looking for a name
a planet to circle a brief sun a shade
a fixture of sand in the midst of a poem
that is being written in cuneiform
just outside the middle of water
how distance creates longing
as it reaches its airy pinnacle
dreaming it is a mortal again
a fringed lunatic with fingers of grass
a small spark before mind comes

**110**

into being and the enormous vision
at the end of the day when mountain
erects its own heaven of sound
echoes of the echo of the soul
vertiginous in its lack of definition
sweet in the decay of time
vanishing in the forever of a vowel
that cannot be pronounced
in the immense eternity
of the imagination

10-31-18

*LIKE NO OTHER DAY*

O bright day of funerals
phantom caravans and trees
bleeding leaves and hands
that carve from useless air
unnamed shadows that haunt
each blade of grass with echoes
of green and russet whisperings
O famous day of burials
interring shadow memories
in myths of earthen make-believe
tops and toys and erector sets
wooden trains that whistle
in windy blasts of Pegasus
small fingers tracing zeroes
in a sleep of stone and moss
O unique day of crematoria
of urns and smoking ash
billowing into the sky's crypt
loud clouds issuing from shells
that once held oceans full
and all the seas of time that

**111**

rush through a dreaming ear
how many the cathedrals
and pyramids of remote light
tumult of a single mountain
turned upside down on its
fragile inch of loss
O wondrous day of mourning
clarity in the second hour
when death becomes
its own receptacle of silence
a glass a dew-drop a sun
whose noon has no hemispheres
distance and solitude
that last the rest of eternity's
sad summer afternoon
O utter day of nothingness
the thing that follows itself
back into fossil night
neither body nor soul
a single string
snapped in discord
between what went before
and what can never
come again

11-01-18


## DIA DE LOS MUERTOS (VIII)
### Max and Joe in tandem

not all the book-learning in the libraries
of the heart can explain the absence of light
though high in his globe of burning azure
the Sun keeps hold of his unruly steeds

**112**

spreading noon across the ruins of night
nor can the spotted god who cares naught
for the circumference of time nor for
the number of steps it takes to climb
either pyramid in dusty Teotihuacan
say anything to bring shadows back from
the sandbanks of illusion at play with dusk
and who can of a late autumn afternoon
sing brightly the lyrics too beautiful in their
protracted grief of echoes and porches and
evenings when the first stars draw diagrams
that the hand falters in its shape of thoughts
and the somewhere of an Hour lacking minutes
is brought to mind of breath slipping away
and telephones and shop windows and toys
elaborate and yet as infinite as the radio
that programs the nocturnal show of life
whispered innuendos dream spun voices
not making sense vowels and bric-a-brac
aphasia the sybilline utterances that map
the hemisphere of mind impossible to discern
planets the size of a dew drop or ink opaque
descents into the other side of the x-ray
so much of this and this and this cannot
be taken away without some purity of flame
some indigo reckoning of yesterdays removed
from the shoe and sleeves empty of winds
and illustrations of the danger of sea-travel
the brain in its microcosm of fireflies flitting
in an organization of cloud and sleep aloft
how distant is everything how out of reach
even the disciples of memory cannot talk
and whatever else the Delphic oracle
or goddess Coatlicue can ever dispel
this one thing is constant this punctuation
of the divine lapse of fingers lost in grass

**113**

of slanted hills and the end of houses
these now faint dots like pauses in space
what can never be obtained the shaking
and puzzlement the obsidian language of
silence

11-02-18

*LIFE ON EARTH*

it was simple it was grace
it was the sum of just so many days
it was light and leaf and branch
it was stone the rock and heights
it was level for just so long
until night came to take its ribbons back
a hill to sleep a cave to dream
a walk through a single summer
a pool a lawn a face that lost its name
it was the circle of morning dew
the vanishing before you could identify
the smallest wonder in the hand
the shape of ink on a paper day
it was a voice from nowhere
or bees and hummingbirds and dragonflies
all but transparent in the water's echo
a place to slip a ground to fall
an evening when doors disappear
it was a house a lamp a floor
it was the window of waking up
a way through woods of no return
it was talking and its silence
a garden of empty vowels
a greenery and a sadness in the brush
it was the child who yearned to run
a pair of knees and shoulders that learn to weep

a longing for other times the undefined
the mind that shaped itself in sleep
it was the letter N or the symbol O
something that could not be understood
a secret inside a word unuttered
a depth in a simple blade of grass
a death in the clod of dirt
it was mourning in the grief of air
a cloud that lingered like a month
moths lit up by lightning and
snatches of conversation in a dream
until night came to take its ribbons back
it was life on earth a minute only
like something seen inside a glass
that has no shape and lacks duration
it was all a dream the passing
between curtains of invisibility
from one bank of the river to the other
it was a memory and that is all
a memory that never was

11-03-18


## ON THE THRESHOLD

I thought I saw someone on the threshold
at four in the morning and dressed
in phantom gear either going forward
or looking back at the life now lost
someone whose head was not on straight
whose shoulders grief laden seemed to shake

out of control emotions signals from on high
legendary phrases or a lunation issuing
from the half-opened mouth someone I
might have known a troubadour or a seer
a person wrapped in mantles of secrecy
a poet perhaps who had given life to
words unknown set to music a spare rhyme
or was it someone closer to me than that
was there a cloister in his appearance
a tower and bells muffled by a passing
or horses yes dusky and slow moving
over a turf of distance and flowing ink
a mourning clap of thunder a distinct echo
of shells the pink orient of the other ear
something else it was and I could not say
the darkest mirror in which myself drowned
in search of contours dust and fragrances
flowers turned to paper and rust in columns
flight of wings in a sudden flutter a song
transparencies of another world asleep
to talk to shadows and adumbrate aloud
the various and fixed planets shifting
in the penumbra as if looking for a number
a cipher a key to unlock the mind's pyramid
but nothing that resembled the light of day
just a figure in disarray in search of
a memory to identify who he could ever be
a stray person gone the relic of a mystery
hands tattooed with invisible alphabets
sweetness of fading autumns in the face
a poetry of bittersweet unreachable hills
and turning again to ascertain and certify
of course was vanished the someone who
hesitated on the threshold between lives
figures and diapason of total silence

Made in the USA
Columbia, SC
17 June 2019